W9-BIW-572

```
223.2      Davis, John J.
DAV            The perfect shepherd.
#7236                                    $4.50
```

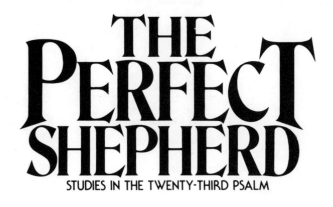

THE PERFECT SHEPHERD

STUDIES IN THE TWENTY-THIRD PSALM

JOHN J. DAVIS

BAKER BOOK HOUSE
Grand Rapids, Michigan

Copyright 1979 by
BMH Books
Winona Lake, Indiana
Reprinted 1980 by
Baker Book House Company

ISBN: 0-8010-2905-8

PHOTOLITHOPRINTED BY CUSHING - MALLOY, INC.
ANN ARBOR, MICHIGAN, UNITED STATES OF AMERICA
1980

To
Earl and Barbara Clark

By the Same Author

Contents

List of Illustrations

9

Foreword

The figure of the shepherd, so familiar to Bible readers, provides rich insights into spiritual truth when its setting is understood. Jesus said, "I am the good shepherd. . . ." (John 10:11). He described His contemporaries as "sheep having no shepherd" (Matt. 9:36) and characterized His mission as a seeking of sheep that were lost (Luke 15:6). These pronouncements become profoundly significant when they are considered in the light of that best-known of the Psalms, which begins, "The Lord is my shepherd" (Psalm 23:1).

Increasing urbanization of this country, however, has made shepherd life a far less conspicuous activity; and many of the connotations which would have immediately come to the minds of those in Bible times may never suggest themselves at all to modern readers. Even sheep raisers on farms and ranches of rural America carry on this occupation quite differently from Palestinian shepherds whose practice was the setting for the Biblical imagery.

Not every attempt to interpret and apply Psalm 23 is as successful as this careful study by my colleague, Dr. John J. Davis. Some books on the Shepherd Psalm are filled with imaginative interpretations that have little basis either in proper exegesis or historical practice among Palestinian shepherds. Dr. Davis possesses that rare combination of skills that makes this volume a reliable source book for every serious and devout reader. His careful scholarship—a product of his many years of teaching the Hebrew text in college and seminary—and his extensive experience in Bible lands, far beyond the superficial acquaintance with Middle East culture that the mere tourist might acquire, radiate from every page. To this is added a sparkling wit, a reverent spirit, an obvious faith in Scripture as God's unique revelation, and a forthright application of these timeless truths that is neither forced nor contrived, but flows directly from the text.

Psalm 23 warms and inspires the heart with a new freshness in the pages of this volume.

Homer A. Kent, Jr.

Preface

In all the poetry of the world there is no passage that equals the charm, beauty and warmth of the Twenty-Third Psalm. It has dried many tears and comforted troubled hearts throughout the ages.

In order to fully appreciate the beauty of this inspired poem, however, one must understand the ways of both shepherd and sheep in Palestine. This little volume is designed to take a careful look at the six verses of the Twenty-Third Psalm against the background of both ancient and modern Palestine. The habits of both shepherd and sheep are carefully studied in order to capture the full message and application of this delightful psalm.

It is hoped that the drawings and photographs will enable the reader to visualize the situations discussed. The principal goal of this study is not merely to glean information about shepherd and sheep, but to better understand the ministry and the majesty of the Shepherd of our souls, the Lord Jesus Christ.

Biblical quotations are normally taken from the Authorized Version, but in a number of instances the author's translation is utilized for discussion. The documentation and bibliography will be of special significance to those students who wish to pursue various matters in greater depth. The concerns of the writer are not only for correct interpretation, but every attempt is made to apply the meaning of these verses to everyday problems and life in general. It is hoped that all who read this volume will be drawn closer to our Shepherd, of whom David spoke so eloquently.

The author wishes to express special appreciation to Dr. John C. Whitcomb, Professor Paulette Sauders, Dr. Charles R. Smith, Dr. Homer A. Kent, Jr., Professor George J. Zemek, Professor Donald L. Fowler, Dr. James R. Battenfield and Miss Nancy Eckert for reading the manuscript and making valuable suggestions as to content and style. Gratitude is also expressed to Mrs. Diane Zuber, who typed the manuscript; and to Dr. Benjamin A. Hamilton, who prepared the indexes. The contributions of all were invaluable and of the highest caliber.

THE PERFECT SHEPHERD

STUDIES IN THE TWENTY-THIRD PSALM

1

The Setting
for the Pearl

This delightfully heart-lifting poem in the divinely inspired Psalter has captivated the imagination of God's people throughout the ages. It breathes calm serenity and a perfect faith. Its impact upon the burdened heart is not due to theological sophistication or philosophical complexity, but to the manner it presents our Shepherd in an unpretentious and simple way.

It has been properly designated the pearl of the Psalms,[1] and its setting in the rugged hills of Palestine serves only to enhance its eternal beauty. A. Maclaren states: "The world could spare many a large book better than this sunny little psalm. It has dried many tears and supplied the mold into which many hearts have poured their peaceful faith."[2]

The worth and impact of this exquisite poem can never be exhausted so long as men, like wandering sheep, need guidance, and so long as they find it in the Lord Jesus, the

Great Shepherd.

This is probably the best-known passage in the Bible—next to the Lord's Prayer. Unfortunately, however, this familiarity has not always produced careful attention to its truths. The psalm brings genuine comfort—but this only comes when one has acquired a personal relationship with the Shepherd. Otherwise, the appropriation of its truth is more psychological and sentimental than spiritual.

I. The Messianic Theme

Psalm 23 is actually part of a messianic trilogy of poems. In the New Testament, the Lord Jesus is referred to as the shepherd in three ways. John 10:11 speaks of Him as the *good shepherd* who gives his life for the sheep. Psalm 22 points to that aspect of His ministry. The words "My God, my God, why hast thou forsaken me?" (v. 1) make it clear that the reference is to the crucified and suffering Messiah. Further we read: "O my God, I cry in the daytime, but thou hearest not; ...." (v. 2). The attitude of the masses is reflected in the seventh verse of that chapter: "All they that see me laugh me to scorn: they shoot out the lip, they shake the head, saying, He trusted on the Lord that he would deliver him: let him deliver him, seeing he delighted in him" (vv. 7-8). The capstone to this identification is the language of verse 18: "They part my garments among them, and cast lots upon my vesture."

It becomes very clear that if one is to assume the full blessings of Psalm 23, he must have a vital encounter with the Good Shepherd of Psalm 22. It is the agony of Calvary that provided the pathway of blessing to green pastures.

The writer of Hebrews has provided a second perspective on the Messiah in describing Him as "... that *great shepherd* of the sheep. ..." (13:20). The greatness of the Shepherd of our souls is no more exquisitely portrayed than in the Twenty-Third Psalm. This clearly emphasizes His present ministry of care and sanctification, thus providing the second member of our poetic trilogy.

Statue of a
shepherd carry-
ing a sheep.
Discovered at
Caesarea.
Photo courtesy
of Homer A.
Kent, Jr.

The Apostle Peter turns our attention to the future with this statement: "And when the *chief Shepherd* shall appear, ye shall receive a crown of glory that fadeth not away" (I Peter 5:4). The glory of the coming Shepherd and the blessing of His own are clearly the emphases of Peter's words. How beautifully this parallels the third aspect of our messianic trilogy in the Psalms. Psalm 24 abounds with praise to the coming King: "Lift up your heads, O ye gates; and be lifted up, ye everlasting doors; and the King of glory shall come in. Who is this King of glory? The Lord strong and mighty, the Lord mighty in battle" (vv. 7-8).

The true believer cannot help but be moved and, in fact, overwhelmed by the implications of these truths. We are His sheep because as the Good Shepherd, He gave Himself for us (John 10:11). It is the Great Shepherd who provides the rich pastures for our present spiritual needs. His power and wisdom enable us to travel right paths and enjoy comfort and peace in the most distressing of moments.

We look forward to the return of that perfect Savior who is the Chief Shepherd. Just as David's outlook reached into the future with the aspiration that he would "dwell in the house of the Lord for ever" (Ps. 23:6), so we cry out for the presence of our Lord and the perfections of heaven.

Psalm 23 appears in Book I of a fivefold division of the Psalter. Evidence points to a rather early date for the division of these books in this manner. Book I consisted of chapters 1-41; Book II, chapters 42-72; Book III, chapters 73-89; Book IV, chapters 90-106; and Book V, chapters 107-150. Each book ends with a doxology (Psalm 150 is the doxology for the final section). This fivefold organization appears to go back as early as the translation of the Septuagint (approximately 200 B.C.), since doxologies appear with the first four books. Testimony to the fivefold division is also preserved in a liturgical fragment from the Dead Sea Scrolls (1Q30).[3]

The reason for this five-book arrangement is not clear. Jewish tradition attributes this organization to an attempt to parallel or "echo" the Pentateuch. Outside the use of the number "five," no real correspondence seems to exist between the Pentateuch and the Psalms. Many writers, however, have attempted to establish such parallelisms. H. C. Leupold argues effectively that " . . . the five books are very closely associated with the gradual growth and development of the whole book. . . ."[4]

A common designation for Books I and II is "Yahwistic Psalter" and "Elohistic Psalter," because the Hebrew divine name *Yahweh* occurs 272 times in Book I (while *Elohim* only 15 times) and the name *Elohim,* 164 times in Book II (whereas *Yahweh* occurs only 30 times). Reasons for these preferences are not clear. Some suggest that this phenomenon reflects an adjustment for liturgical needs, while others view this as a common tendency to substitute the name *Yahweh* for other names.[5] It will be observed that the psalm we are considering falls in Book I—the so-called "Yahwistic Psalter." It is of interest that the divine name employed by the writer of Psalm is *Yahweh*—that special covenant name.

II. Spirit of Hebrew Poetry

We would be negligent if we did not take a look at the immediate literary context of our psalm. It certainly is not necessary to labor the fact of the importance of the Psalter in the development of a Christian theology, as well as the suggestions of practical truth. The poetry of the Psalms expresses the spontaneous overflow of powerful emotion generated by God's great blessing. In order to fully understand the experience of the Old Testament saint, one must live through times of extreme ecstasy as well as days of despair and disappointment. These experiences are expertly reflected in the literature of the Psalter. But one must remember that the Psalms are more than mere emotional expressions; they are the vehicle of divine revelation in the fullest sense (II Tim. 3:16). To study the Psalms is to allow oneself to become better acquainted with the heart and soul of the Old Testament saint. There are a number of things that characterize the spirit and content of Hebrew poetry.

Shepherds at Bethlehem. Levant Photo Service.

A. Intense Theism. In the Psalms, the question of God's existence is never raised. In fact, those who harbor ideas which deny His existence are classified as fools (Ps. 14:1). The psalmists had at their disposal the Pentateuch and subsequent revelation which declared and described the creative activity of God. The complexity, beauty and power of the created universe were evidences enough for the writers that this declaration was true. It might be noted that as they could not find adequate explanation for the origin of the universe apart from a living, powerful God after 2,000 years of philosophical and scientific inquiry, we still have no reasonable explanation for our world—apart from divine creation.

We live in an extremely skeptical age that, in many respects, has deified natural science. Materialistic minds continue to challenge God to prove His existence by a special act or by visible appearance. Whenever I read or hear such challenges, I am reminded of the fable of the little red ant which arduously climbed on top of one of the rails of the Seaboard Coast Line Railroad in Florida. It stood up on its legs and denied the existence of the railroad president. The ant confidently asserted that it had not seen this president nor had a scientific encounter with him. "If he really exists," the ant said, "let him come down and squash me on the rail." It is somewhat ironic that some of the world's most bitter critics are the ones sitting on the most obvious evidence. But, you say, if God does exist, why doesn't He answer His critics? My answer is simply that it is for the same reason that the president of the Seaboard Coast Line Railroad will not make a trip all the way to Florida just to squash a little ant and satisfy its curiosity. The God whom I worship is much greater than all that. Modern man, like the psalmist of old, needs only to look at the beauty and the awesome power of nature to see the hand of God.

I've often wanted to invite an atheist for a special dinner in my home and then inquire afterward if he thought there was a cook.

The constant emphasis of the poets in the Psalms is upon the character and the attributes of God. This theme is woven with a variety of moods, literary styles and terms. With amazing skill, the writers blend God's transcendence and power with His immanent presence. In our day, as in the past, we have seen the transcendence of God taken to such

23

extremes that He is depersonalized. On the other extreme are pop theologians who have reduced God to the level of mere sinful man and stripped Him of His glory. While David was able to see the great power of God exercised in creation and providence, he also, with simple faith, appropriated the tender presence of a loving shepherd.

B. A Unique View of Man. The Psalms stand uniquely alone among the poetic literatures of the ancient world in their description of man, his character and destiny. They approach the subject of man with a blunt realism and view his activities in the light of God's absolute holiness. The Psalms' view of man is quite complete as they see him in all of his basic relationships (e.g., with God, man, nature, and so on). While poets and other writers of more modern years have tended to praise man for his great achievements, the psalmist views man in the light of God's magnificent creation and finds it incredible that the Lord should even consider him. Note this declaration: "When I consider thy heavens, the work of thy fingers, the moon and the stars, which thou hast ordained: what is man, that thou art mindful of him? and the son of man, that thou visitest him?" (Ps. 8:3-4).

One of the most significant contributions of the Psalter is its view of sin and sin's effects upon man. Man is seen as a fallen sinful creature in need of divine redemption. The agony and despair that sin produces are constant emphases of all the writers. The psalmist often bares the complexities of his own soul, including very pointed statements about his disappointments, as well as his delights. Just as the psalmist describes the awful destructive effects of sin, so he delights to emphasize the beauty and the victory wrought by God's redemption.

C. Simplicity and Naturalness. One of the striking features of the Psalter is its communication of great and complex truths with the simplest of illustrations and ideas. Along with the theological uniqueness of these writings, this certainly is a mark of inspiration. Theological communication is often cumbersome and burdened with complex terms and expressions. Even with modern vocabularies and all their refinements, we have yet to exceed the beauty and simplicity of the Psalter's expressions. It is perhaps this feature that provides the basis for the universal adaptability and appeal of the Psalms. There is poetic freedom, but not at the expense of beautiful standard literary patterns.

D. Enduring Charm. Even though the material of the Psalter, like that of other portions of Scripture, is culturally conditioned, it is not restrictive. Its wisdom is practical and universal. The problems and emotions described in the Psalms are the very problems and emotions encountered by people of all ages in all lands. It is that feature that has enhanced its charm and impact.

When one considers the universal appeal of the Psalms and their continued use, he becomes even more convinced of their divine inspiration. Modern archaeological activity in various countries of the Near East has produced volumes of ancient poetic literature. Much of this literature is religious and mythical, but was buried in the dust of destruction. The Biblical Psalms alone were preserved in use, and bear a special impact upon the hearts of believing people. Surely, against this background, we must call them unique and of special importance. The unwavering monotheism of the writers coupled with their warm expressions of love for the Lord stand out in bold relief.

III. Creation Perspectives

Some have charged that the ancient Hebrews lacked a truly aesthetic sense; but one cannot read the lofty and sensitive poetic expressions of the Psalter and draw that conclusion.

Both the book of Job and the book of Psalms contain a number of nature poems, for the majesty and sublimity of nature moved the poets of Israel to poetical outbursts. Many are the descriptions of the beauty of the flowers and the fragrance of the trees; of the storms passing over the Mediterranean Sea and the plains of Bashan. The glories of creation, the snowcapped mountains and the flower-covered fields have also touched the hearts and fired the imagination of the Hebrew Psalmists. They were struck and over-awed by the immensity of nature and saddened by the insignificance of man as compared to it.[6]

One has only to listen to the songs of exaltation to recognize the love that the poets had for natural beauty and for the God who produced it: "The pastures are clothed with flocks; the valleys also are covered over with corn. . . [Nature is rejuvenated], sings and shouts for joy" (Ps. 65:13). Such expressions of joy and pleasure characterize visions of calm waters, beautiful valleys and lush pastures.

In contrast to these joyful observations, however, are the awesome thunderings of the storms and the billows which reminded the psalmists of God's great power. "The voice of the Lord is upon the waters: the God of glory thundereth. . . . The voice of the Lord breaketh the cedars; yea, the Lord breaketh [in pieces] the cedars of Lebanon. The voice of the Lord divideth [cleaveth] the flames of fire. The voice of the Lord shaketh the wilderness. . . ." (Ps. 29:3, 5, 7, 8). "Bow thy heavens, O Lord, and come down: touch the mountains, and they shall smoke" (Ps. 144:5). These are not superficial, throbbing passions for nature itself, but are songs of praise directed to the Creator. If creation exhibits such awesome power and overwhelming beauty, what must the Creator Himself be like? We, along with the writers, stand in awe at such a contemplation.

It has been this writer's privilege on many occasions to spend quiet evenings in the hills of Judah. When darkness sets in, there are no street lights, smog or other distractions to mar the staggering beauty of the heavens. It is no wonder that the psalmist cried out: "The heavens declare the glory of God; and the firmament sheweth his handywork" (Ps. 19:1). I can recall with an ever-deepening sense of awe the amazing beauty of the heavens. The uncluttered skies of Palestine seemed saturated with magnificent starry clusters that were just inches beyond my reach. The uninterrupted silence of those hills, coupled with the mind-boggling beauty of the heavens, very quickly turned my attention to the God of the universe. In a very special sense, that is precisely what Psalm 23 does, but with a different approach.

Elsewhere in the Psalms, the writers alluded to the Lord as their shield, sword, rock, and so forth. Such associations are important, but they lack the beauty of the shepherd metaphor. These impersonal things do not create the impact for personal response that the relationship of a shepherd to his sheep encourages.

It is not difficult to ascertain the reasons for the popularity of Psalm 23. It is universally loved for its simplicity, realism and brevity. It will be our task to discover its meaning and to seek effective applications of its truth.

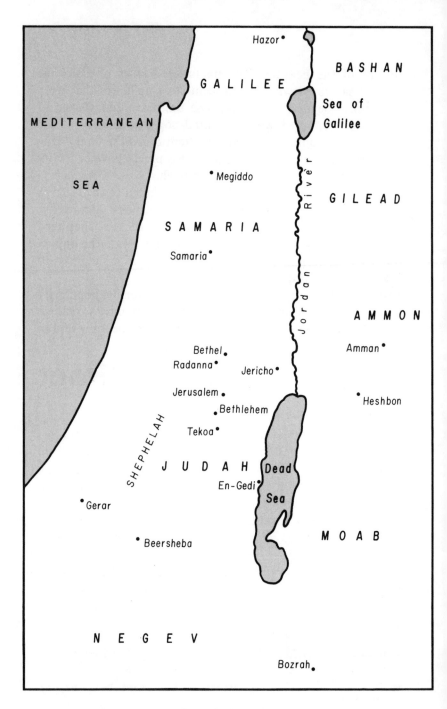

The land of Palestine

2

The Inspired Poet

The intriguing beauty of this shepherd psalm has attracted the attention of many literary analysts. While the studies of such writers have been interesting and informative, many fall short of the mark in true interpretation because they fail to recognize that this is more than a mere poem. It is divine revelation. The profound and lasting serenity of this poem cannot be explained on mere literary grounds. The feeling of confidence the psalm produces is a product of God's creative breath. We are reminded by the Apostle Paul that all Scripture is "God breathed" (II Tim. 3:16).

I. The Author

It has been fashionable among many critics to divide this psalm among a number of authors living anywhere from the early post-Solomonic age down to the Maccabean period.

The apparent change in metaphorical expression between verses 4 and 5 is for some an indicator of multiple authorship.

The reference to "the house of the Lord" in the sixth verse is regarded by many to be a direct reference to the temple, which of course was not constructed until after David's death. On that basis, authorship has been attributed to unknown writers of a later period of time.

There is really no adequate reason for denying the authorship of this psalm to David. The Hebrew title to the poem is *mizmôr lᵉdāwid* ("a song of praise by David"). While it is true that the Hebrew preposition *lāmed* can merely mean "about" or "belonging to," it also can be a proper designation for authorship or origin.[1] The term *mizmôr* ("song, psalm") has reference to a song rendered to the accompaniment of instrumental music. The term is used 57 times in psalm titles and is derived from the root *zāmar,* meaning "to pluck." The reference is to the plucking of stringed instruments.[2]

In the minds of many, the title itself would not be sufficient evidence for Davidic authorship. The historical reliability of these titles has often been questioned, but in this case (as in the case of most of the titles) there is little reason to doubt their historical reliability. The title, coupled with the internal data of the psalm and the historical circumstances of David's life, make his authorship the most attractive conclusion.

In II Samuel 23:1 David is designated, "the sweet psalmist of Israel." One of the things that attracted Saul to David was the fact that he was "cunning [skilled] in playing" (I Sam. 16:18). When the Spirit of God had departed from Saul and he suffered, David was called upon to play the harp—thus soothing the distressed soul of Israel's condemned king (I Sam. 16:23). David performed for Saul at least twice in the royal court, and on both occasions barely escaped with his life. In I Samuel 18:10, we are told that an evil spirit from God had come upon Saul—and David provided music in hope that the crisis in Saul's life would pass. But, either due to David's selection of music (he may have given a rendition of the number 1 tune of the day, "Saul hath slain his thousands, and David his ten thousands"—I Sam. 18:7) or, more likely, to the fact that Saul despised David's popularity, Saul sought this occasion to take David's life. What I have always found utterly amazing is that David returned to the royal court for a repeat performance (I Sam. 19:10). Once again, David was able to escape the javelin of Saul, but one can only speculate what the palace wall must have looked like after this activity! There is, therefore, very little question about David's musical skill and his capability as a poet.[3]

Furthermore, the fact that David spent his boyhood as a shepherd would provide a very natural background for the type of expression encountered in Psalm 23. He not only cared for his father's sheep, but was very successful in their defense. According to I Samuel 17:34-35, he slew both a lion and a bear in defense of the flock. If Goliath had only known this, he may have been more modest in his taunts! While it is true that most writers of the ancient world could use shepherding as an analogy in the general sense, it seems that this psalm includes the kind of detail and mode of expression that would come from one who had *experienced* the events of shepherding rather than just having observed them.

II. The Date

Since many writers have chosen to deny Davidic authorship and ascribe the psalm to one or more later authors, it should not be surprising that some dates range as late as the post-exilic period. For example, Taylor and McCullough confidently assert that "the individualism of the Psalm points to a date in the post-exilic period. . . ."[4] Others feel the psalm belongs to a time period when the temple was in existence, but prior to the exile.[5] The early monarchial period is a favorite date for the greater majority of writers, however.[6]

The best evidence seems to point to Davidic authorship and a date of composition late in his life. A popular view is that at least part of the psalm was composed during the time of Absalom's rebellion.[7] It is suggested that his own shepherd

Sheep in the hills of Judah. Levant Photo Service.

experience provided the images and language of the first four verses. The circumstances of Absalom's rebellion, which required David to go to Mahanaim where he and his friends were cared for by the kindness of Barzillai and other friends, provided the background for the remaining verses of the psalm. The above suggestions are clearly possible, but it is not necessary to trace this psalm to particular events in David's life. His many years as a shepherd and the great protection and care of God in his life through a number of circumstances would be sufficient reason for him to write a poem of this nature.

III. The Images

The debate over the number of metaphors in the psalm has

been lively and continues to occupy the minds of those studying this portion of Scripture. There are four basic views as to the number of metaphors employed by the writer. One suggestion is that the entire psalm is devoted to the shepherd-sheep image.[8] While many have found this an attractive approach, there are serious difficulties with relating the language of verse 5 to this background. For example, in what way would sheep feed at a "table" as a normal part of their activity? Phillip Keller's attempt to relate the word "table" to the high plateau of the sheep ranges in western United States and southern Europe is a bit strained. He notes that the Spanish word used for these pastures is *mesas* ("tables").[9] The context for Psalm 23 is not western ranch-type sheepherding, however, but the Oriental pastoral life, which differs in many significant aspects—including the terrain. Psalm 23 must be properly viewed within its Oriental-Palestinian context rather than according to the ranching methods and techniques of the modern West.

Another problem connected with the single figure view is the presence of the "cup" in verse 5. This has often been identified with the stone-cut trough that one finds next to many cisterns in Palestine. This is a possible association, but, as we shall see later, it is probably not the preferred one.

The most common interpretation of this psalm is that there are two basic metaphors employed. Verses 1 through 4 portray the activities of a shepherd, while verses 5 and 6 are descriptive of a gracious host and his guest.[10] Without question, this is the most widely accepted interpretation of the figures. The transition from shepherding life to the gracious host is not introduced. It is felt that such transitions are not uncommon in Hebrew poetry. The use of the expressions "table" and "cup" most easily fit into this context.

A third suggestion regarding the imagery of the psalm is that there are three different pictures included. W. Graham Scroggie[11] and J. Sidlow Baxter[12] see the images of the shepherd and sheep (vv. 1-2), the guide and traveler (vv. 3-4), and the host and the guest (vv. 5-6). This approach to the psalm is not widely accepted, due probably to the rather forced nature of the created image in verses 3 and 4. The transition from shepherd and sheep to pilgrim and guide seems rather unnecessary since the activities of verses 3 and 4 are perfectly natural for shepherd and sheep.

P. Volz, on the other hand, sees four images in the psalm: shepherd, leader, host and father of the house.[13] This approach to the images seems rather unnecessary and tends to fragment the psalm beyond reasonable proportion.

From all the evidence in the text at hand, it would seem that the psalm contains one metaphor with two aspects. It seems to this writer that it is possible to combine several elements of the above views for a more preferred approach. It is possible that David was viewing the shepherd throughout the psalm, but in two different roles. In verses 1 through 4, he sees the shepherd in direct relationship to pastoral activities and his care for the sheep. In verses 5 and 6, the shepherd is viewed as a gracious Oriental host at his large tent where he cares for his guests during a dinner or banquet. We shall return to these possibilities later in our studies.

While most people are familiar, at least in a general sense, with the activities of the shepherd and sheep, it should not be assumed that this subject is quickly exhausted with a mere survey of that relationship. I have the privilege of reading through this psalm in the Hebrew text with a large number of students at Grace Theological Seminary every year. I find the Twenty-Third Psalm like moving water that begins as a small stream, but the more one traces its path, it continues to widen into a river, and ultimately an overwhelming ocean of spiritual truth. It would be tragic indeed if we merely outlined the course of that river and never took time to drink for refreshment. The incredible beauty and spiritual wealth of this poem will never be fully exhausted, simply because its focus is on the Good Shepherd, who is the Lord Himself.

3

The Shepherd

Psalm 23:1

While the voice of David and the strings of his harp have been silent for 3,000 years, the songs of praise penned by this inspired man continue to linger on and move the hearts of God's people.

David's selection of the shepherd-sheep relationship to illustrate the benefits of God's grace was most appropriate; first, because he knew by experience the great challenges, dangers, and joys of pastoring large flocks. And second, he understood the thrill of a personal relationship with the Lord, the Shepherd of Israel.

My various travels to Jordan, Egypt and Israel have brought me into numerous contacts with shepherds and their flocks. On one occasion, having completed archaeological work at ancient Tekoa, I had the privilege of spending a week with a shepherd and his sheep as they made their way from Tekoa eastward to En-Gedi. Mohammad Yaseen had approximately 75 sheep and 30 goats in his flock. We talked one day concerning the responsibilities and the burdens of the shepherd. I told him it was my desire to learn as much as I possibly could about the life of a shepherd. His response was surprising and caught me off guard.

"Dr. Davis, if you wish to know a shepherd, you shall become one and be with me this next week." That statement produced moments of silence and a somewhat blank look on my face. After I gathered my thoughts and remembered that the next seven or eight days would be free, I joyfully responded, "I'd be delighted to work with you and learn the ways of the shepherd."

The days that followed in the wilderness of Judah provided some of the richest experiences of my life and the foundation for new insights into my relationship with the Lord. I might also add that it had no small number of surprises for this westerner who, though familiar with the rugged woods of the north in hunting and fishing, was not quite prepared for some of the challenges of a Judaean wilderness.

One of the first things insisted upon by Mohammad was a change of attire. We went to his tent and he was able to secure some clothing, including a larger outer cloak that I should carry with me. The work shoes I was wearing seemed unnecessary to him and he recommended the traditional sandals. At first this seemed like a perfectly logical move in the light of the coolness and the potential comfort that these would provide. Three days' experience through the wadis and mountainsides proved this to be a mistake. My feet had not developed the leather-like base that his had, and the blisters, combined with thorns and stones, made for some agonizing travel. I was sure, upon stopping one day, that I saw smoke coming out of the bottom of the sandals—from the intense desert heat!

The travels with Mohammad also provided some very practical experience in wilderness journeying. After approximately three and one-half hours of travel through narrow wadis, along trails and around hills, we decided to

Caring for thirsty sheep. Matson Photo Service.

stop for some rest near a small cave. In spite of my belief that I was in outstanding condition—after an archaeological season and hard work in the field—I found that such travel had its own unique challenges. Weary and not particularly cognizant of my immediate surroundings, I decided to sit down and rest for a time. Not carefully checking the rock on which I was going to sit, I found myself settling upon a one-inch buck thorn, which produced a vertical ascent that exceeded any of my other movements during that day, both in zeal and velocity! Mohammad found himself in tears with laughter; for me, it was a very pointed lesson!

Our travels and times of rest provided many occasions for discussion concerning the shepherd and his responsibilities. Four principal ideas emerged as essential elements of a good shepherd. Later, when I considered Biblical perspectives on this subject, I was amazed to note that all of the areas emphasized were precisely the same concerns of the Bible.

I. The Shepherd as a Man

A good shepherd is a knowledgeable man. He knows his own capabilities and strengths. Perhaps equally important, he knows the terrain over which he must travel and feed his sheep. My travels with some of the shepherds of Judah convinced me that this is an all-important quality of a good shepherd. The rugged hills, the distant water places and the difficulty in finding adequate pasture all pointed to the need for accurate knowledge on the part of the shepherd.

He must also know the sheep. Without being aware of their capabilities and limitations, he could easily destroy the flock through overdriving them (Gen. 33:13). He needs to know the number of sheep under his care and check on that number constantly. For if a sheep or goat should wander away for any length of time, it might die of starvation in the desert or be devoured by a wild animal. It is no accident that the Lord Jesus said, "I know my own, and mine own know me" (John 10:14). Throughout that lovely tenth chapter of the Gospel of John, the knowledge and the love of a good shepherd are highlighted.

While sitting on the hillside one night watching the sheep in a small sheepfold, Mohammad and I talked about some of the attitudes of a shepherd. He constantly mentioned the fact that the best shepherds are those who genuinely love their sheep. They not only should love them, but should feel deep obligation for their care and growth. "It is this," Mohammad emphasized, "that causes a shepherd to be willing to give his life in the protection of sheep."

We remember well that the Lord Jesus expressed the fact

Helmi Musa gives special attention to an injured lamb. Photo by the author.

that He loves His sheep. The Father has given them into His hand and He has assumed their feeding and protection. What a comfort there is in the fact that the shepherd of our souls is none other than the sovereign Lord.

The shepherd encounters many dangers while guiding his flocks and caring for them during pasturing. It really takes courage to assume the responsibility and the care for large flocks of sheep and goats. Before traveling with Mohammad, I had a very romanticized concept of the shepherd and his relationship with the sheep. A couple of nights in the wilderness and some oppressive days in the desert brought me to a confrontation with practical realities. Jacob reminded Laban of some of these difficulties: "Thus I was; in the day the drought consumed me, and the frost by night; and my sleep departed from mine eyes" (Gen. 31:40).

There are, of course, the ever-present quantities of flies that irritate sheep, goats and shepherd alike. Add to this the scratches and scrapes that come from walking in rocky regions, through helping injured animals whose dispositions become irritable and whose wounds fester rather than heal even with medication. Great courage is also needed because rugged territories through which shepherds often must go are perfect hiding places for the robber or the wild animal.

It became apparent that the shepherd needs to be a man of strength. The rigor of moving through that territory, at times carrying injured animals, puts a very special demand on the shepherd. Isaiah described his duties in this manner: "He shall feed his flock like a shepherd: he shall gather the lambs with his arm, and carry them in his bosom, and shall gently lead those that are with young" (Isa. 40:11).

The exercise of such strength, my friends, is not the glamorous, picturesque, stained glass representations we see in many of our beautiful cathedrals and churches. To carry a sheep or a lamb is a difficult task. The weight, irritability, smell and the ever-present flies on that animal make the task one of real challenge. Only courage and strength, coupled with special love, enables the shepherd to endure the inconvenience of such activity.

Strength is also required in the recovery of wandering sheep. On one occasion, we had to rescue a small lamb that had wandered down a cliff and was perched on a precipice overlooking a 300-foot drop. Only the most delicate of movements made it possible for Mohammad to snatch the lamb from impending death. His courage and skill in the rescue of that sheep was reminiscent of Jesus' parable in which he asked: "What man of you, having an hundred sheep, if he lose one of them, doth not leave the ninety and nine in the wilderness, and go after that which is lost, until he find it? And when he hath found it, he layeth it on his shoulders, rejoicing" (Luke 15:4-5).

Wisdom is also a necessary characteristic of a successful shepherd. The mere exercise of brute strength is not the final solution to the needs of the sheep. It might be courageous for me to jump into the ring with a world champion heavyweight boxer like Muhammad Ali, but it clearly would illustrate the total absence of wisdom! A good shepherd will not take unnecessary chances with his flocks. He will judiciously avoid impending dangers and confrontations that could jeopardize the lives of his sheep, as well as his own.

Needless to say, it takes great wisdom to effectively care for large flocks. In the Old Testament, some flocks numbered as many as 7,000 (Job 1:3) and 3,000 (I Sam. 25:2). In the case of such numbers, there were probably under-shepherds who were hired to assist the shepherd and to maintain a proper count of the sheep and goats.

In addition to the wisdom required of a shepherd, the practical attribute of dependability is always necessary. Shepherding is a 24-hour commitment. I cannot remember seeing sizable flocks of sheep and goats wandering without the presence of a shepherd. Remember that when young David went before King Saul and offered his services to challenge Goliath, his older brother Eliab immediately asked, ". . . with whom hast thou left those few sheep in the wilderness? . . . ." (I Sam. 17:28).

When a shepherd assumes the task of caring for a flock of sheep and goats, he also assumes great liability for those animals. In the context of the ancient Near East, shepherds had various relationships, both to the owner of the flock (if they did not personally own it) and to the flock itself. He might have owned the flock himself, or he may well have been hired by a wealthy man to care for the flock. If the flock were large, under-shepherds would be utilized as well. The shepherd accepted personal liability for the flocks and was remunerated in proportion to the growth of the flock and the amount of its produce. We know from ancient documents that such an arrangement provided a strong incentive for the shepherd to promote the welfare of the animals.

In Babylon and elsewhere, it was customary for annual agreements to be drawn up between flock-owners and shepherds. At the end of each year, the shepherd would have to give an account of all the sheep under his care. He, of course, was not held responsible for the animals which died naturally during the year. It was customary for a shepherd to skin those animals and then present their skins, with the wool and probably also some of the tendons, as proof to their owner that the animals had not been sold or lost through negligence.[1] If a shepherd lost a sheep and, therefore, was unable to produce the skin, he was obliged to replace it with another animal.[2] According to Exodus 22:12, if an animal was stolen from him, he was required to make restitution to the owner—which might be payment or the replacement of the animal. This was also the requirement specified in the law code of Hammurabi.[3]

Jacob reminded Laban of his dependability: "This twenty years have I been with thee; thy ewes and thy she goats have not cast their young, and the rams of thy flock have I not eaten. That which was torn of beasts I brought not unto thee; I bare the loss of it; of my hand didst thou require it, whether stolen by day, or stolen by night" (Gen. 31:38-39). Dependability and faithfulness, therefore, were not secondary characteristics of a good shepherd.

II. The Shepherd as Provider

One of the most well-known responsibilities of the shepherd, and certainly one highlighted in Psalm 23, is his responsibility to find adequate water and pasturage for his flocks (Gen. 4:20; 13:2-6, 11, 18).

Perhaps the clearest passage on the importance of this responsibility is Ezekiel's prophecy against the "shepherds" of Israel (Ezek. chapter 34). The Lord cried out: " . . . Woe be to the shepherds of Israel that do feed themselves! Should not the shepherds feed the flocks? Ye eat the fat, and ye clothe you with the wool, ye kill them that are fed: but ye feed not the flock" (Ezek. 34:2-3).[4] The Lord promised: "I will feed them in a good pasture, and upon the high mountains of Israel shall their fold be: there shall they lie in a good fold, and in a fat pasture shall they feed upon the mountains of Israel" (Ezek. 34:14).

It might be pointed out here that, spiritually speaking, those charged by God to lead His flock are likewise responsible for providing adequate food. This was clear in the indictments of the Lord through Ezekiel. A similar emphasis is found in Micah 7:14. "Feed thy people with thy rod, the flock of thine heritage. . . ." If Peter were to render true service to the Lord through love, he was expected to feed the sheep and the lambs of the Lord (cf. John 21:15-17).

One suspects that at the Judgment Seat of Christ, there will be many "shepherds" or "pastors" who will be held accountable for having failed to nourish the people of God through the meat and the milk of His Word. Far too many pass through the doors of churches with pain-producing hunger, only to have stubble and thorns thrown at their feet in the form of pithy platitudes and poetic niceties, garnished with some moral generalities.

III. The Shepherd as Protector

Wolves, lions, bears and jackals were some of the animals with which the shepherd had to contend in ancient Palestine.

Palestinian sheepfold. Photo by: Homer A. Kent, Jr.

On two occasions, David had to rescue lambs that had been seized by a lion and a bear (I Sam. 17:34-35). Of course, David recognized that it was the living God who gave him strength to overcome these animals (I Sam. 17:37).[5]

Shelter for the night was also part of the provisions expected of the shepherd. In Palestine, the sheep are usually gathered and kept in circular, stone sheepfolds. Or, on occasion, they may be gathered into a cave, with the shepherd guarding the entrance. Many times, a shepherd on the move will make a hastily erected enclosure of thorny bushes and shrubbery, but where he remains for a period of time, the sheepfold usually consists of a stone enclosure (cf. Num. 32:16). Frequently, the shepherd will top these walls with the branches of thorny shrubs in order to keep the sheep in and to discourage wild animals on the outside.

It might be well to pause for reflection on the imagery found in John 10:7-9 at this point. Many have been bothered by the apparent harsh change in the figure from a shepherd to the door of a sheepfold. In my experiences with Abas Tawfeek, a young, but highly skilled shepherd, in southern Jordan, we learned of some habits that shed light on this problem. We had just gathered the sheep and driven them into a typical circular sheepfold not far from a village, and were preparing to settle down for the night. Abas made the most fascinating statement, "You may sleep in the corner of the sheepfold where there is a small wall, so the sheep will not bother you. I will be the door." So it appears, in this instance at least, he was both the shepherd and door; and perhaps this is the sense of John's allusions to Christ's ministry.

I have since discovered that this has been the experience of other observers as well. Dr. William M. Miller relates this experience:

> Many years ago I was traveling by donkey from Mishapur, the city of the poet Omar Khayyam, in eastern Iran to Sabsevar a three days' journey to the west. We stopped in a tiny village of mud huts for the night, and when we arose next morning, the dry, dusty land was covered with a mantle of beautiful white snow.
>
> As the donkey driver stated firmly that it was impossible for his animals to move while the snow as so deep, there was nothing to do but wait till the snow melted a bit. So all that day we remained in the village.
>
> In the afternoon, I set out to see the sights about the village. Not far away, I came to a mound of earth piled up in a large circle, like a crude rampart, and on the top of the mound all around the circle was a heap of dry thorns. As I stood wondering what this might be, one of the villagers approached me. "Salaam," I said, "Please tell me what this enclosure is for."
>
> "Oh, that is for the sheep," he replied. "They are brought in here for the night for safety."
>
> "Good," I said, "but why have the dry thorns been piled on top of the wall?"
>
> "That," he replied, "is a protection against wolves. If a wolf

tries to break in and attack the sheep, he will knock against the thorns, and they will make a noise, and the shepherd will wake up, and drive off the wolf."

"That is fine," I said, "but why does the wolf try to climb over the wall? Here is the entrance to the enclosure, it is open. There is no door to keep out the wolf; he could easily enter here."

"Oh, no," said my guide, "you do not understand. That is where the shepherd sleeps. The shepherd is the door."[6]

There was a time when some critics had serious doubts about the presence of large carnivorous animals in Palestine. Archaeological research in the past 50 years has pretty much decimated such critical ideas. Scientific field analysis today includes the careful study of animal bones as well as all other data retrievable at an archaeological site. The excellent work done at Tel Ḥesbân is an example of this type of activity.

Analyzing ancient animal bones at the Heshbon Archaeological Expedition. Andrews University Expedition to Tell Hisban, Paul H. Denton, photographer.

A limestone relief from the 5th Dynasty tomb of TJI, Sakkarah, Egypt. From The Symbolism of the Biblical World by Othmar Keel. Seabury Press, publishers.

Mammals recovered during the 1976 expedition included the fox, badger, weasel, marbled polecat, hyena wildcat and the lion.[7]

One of the real dangers to the shepherd and his flocks is the thief, who has roamed the rugged hills of Palestine from the most ancient of times. Mohammad Yaseen remarked a number of times that the thief is one of his great fears. The shepherd is very vulnerable because of the deep wadis and passes through which he must go. Raids on flocks of sheep and goats are still common in the eastern deserts of Jordan. Often this leads to open warfare between various nomadic groups. W. M. Thomson's account of the death of one shepherd best illustrates the point.

> And when the thief and the robber come (and come they do), the faithful shepherd has often to put his life in his hand to defend the flock. I have known more than one case in which he had literally to lay it down in the contest. A faithful fellow last spring, between Tiberias and Tabor, instead of fleeing, actually fought three Bedawin robbers until he was hacked to

pieces with their Khanjars, and died among the sheep he was defending.[8]

A number of Arabs have related the grim stories of the deaths of shepherds in the wilderness. Some were shot by marauding bandits who would take the number of sheep desired and then flee, unchallenged by anyone else. This fact became a depressing reality when Mohammad Yaseen showed me a place next to a valley where he had personally covered over the remains of a bedouin shepherd who had been shot in defense of his sheep. Many times the shepherds were aided in defense of these flocks with one or more dogs. These dogs are often quite large and are vicious fighters.

Contemplation of the protective qualities of our Shepherd can only bring comfort and joy. In spite of the awesome nature of our enemies, we can take comfort in these promises: "And I give unto them eternal life; and they shall never perish, neither shall any man pluck them out of my hand. My Father, which gave them [to] me, is greater than all; and no man is able to pluck them out of my Father's hand" (John 10:28-29).

IV. The Shepherd as a Guide

One of the amazing discoveries of my days with Palestinian shepherds was the ability of these men to lead their flocks through the most difficult of places. They always seemed to know the safety of the trail and the best and most efficient way to get to pastures and adequate water supplies. It is well known, of course, that Palestinian shepherds normally *lead* their sheep rather than *drive* them. The intimate relationship sustained between shepherd and sheep makes this possible. Herein lies a big difference between ranching techniques of the West and the personalized intimate relationship established in the Oriental East.

On many occasions I have seen one or two shepherds approach a large flock of sheep grazing on a hillside. The one shepherd will begin to walk away from the large flock and give an ear-piercing cry which signals his own sheep to follow him. Amazingly, these sheep will begin to move out of the flock and follow that shepherd. Each shepherd seems to have his own special call or voice intonation that has been impressed in the consciousnesses of those sheep, and they immediately follow.

Some of the sheep are distinctive in their markings and often bear a special relationship to the shepherd. Both Mohammad Yaseen and Abas Tawfeek, as well as other shepherds with whom I have traveled, had favorite sheep or goats to whom they had given names. This imagery is utilized by our Lord to explain the unique relationship His flock has to Him.

> To him the porter openeth; and the sheep hear his voice: and he calleth his own sheep by name, and leadeth them out. And when he putteth forth his own sheep, he goeth before them, and the sheep follow him: for they know his voice. And a stranger will they not follow, but will flee from him: for they know not the voice of strangers (John 10:3-5).

If we find comfort in the Palestinian shepherd because of his amazing knowledge of the terrain and ability to successfully guide flocks of sheep through the narrow places to the plush pastures, how much more should a child of God rejoice in the infinitely complete knowledge of the Chief Shepherd who knows not only the present, but also the past and future—to perfection. He not only leads us, but leads us in the right paths and this for the glory of His name.

V. The Lord as Shepherd (Psalm 23:1)

With this background in mind, it now behooves us to listen to the first string of David's magnificent harp. In the Hebrew text, the first verse consists of only four words, but how rich and full those words are. Literally translated they read: "The Lord (Yahweh) is my shepherd, I will not have need." It is no accident that the divine name is first in the sentence and, therefore, in an emphatic position. The name *Yahweh* is

49

based on the Hebrew verb *hāyâ* meaning "to be." This name is an assertion of the Lord's self-existence. Simply translated it would be, "He is." It was this name that was revealed to Moses in Exodus 3:14. Jesus identified Himself with this name when He consistently spoke of Himself as the great "I Am."

The first verse emphasizes the *provisions for the sheep.* Whatever the sheep enjoy comes as a result of divine blessing. The rest of this verse and the rest of the chapter have no significant impact apart from the identity of the Lord of the flock. It is the character, the power and the eternal nature of this Matchless One that makes the blessings of the pastures and streams possible.

It should also be observed that the name *Yahweh* was that special covenant name for the Lord in the Old Testament (Exod. 6:3). David had a special appreciation for the covenant aspects of the name for the Lord made a covenant with David which promised that ". . . thine house and thy kingdom shall be established for ever. . . ." (II Sam. 7:16). While certainly disappointed in being denied the privilege of building the great temple, David nonetheless rejoiced in the great covenant promises of his God. In the worship and the prayer that followed, that divine name is emphatically praised (II Sam. 7:18-19).

When David, therefore, speaks of the Lord as his shepherd, he is emphasizing the inexhaustible resources available to the sheep. On the other hand, when the weaknesses and ineptitude of the sheep are considered, the name *Yahweh* emphasizes the indispensable nature of that relationship. In the light of John 10 and the sovereign power of the shepherd, the indivisible aspects of this relationship are also included.

The second word in the original text is *rōᶜî* and is translated, "my shepherd." The word is related to the Hebrew verb *rāᶜâ* which simply means, "to feed, graze, or pasture." In the light of the shepherd's responsibilities and capabilities, one can see the vast potential and prospect of the Lord being a shepherd. However, the intimacy of the psalm is not reflected in that impersonal theological assertion. The real impact of the psalm is in the addition of the personal pronoun, "my." It is this appropriation that makes the psalm so attractive and comforting. This association is not established by superficial acclamation, but by a forthright encounter with the suffering shepherd of Psalm 22. Only those who have met the Lord on Mount Calvary can expect the delightful pastures of His unique blessing. It is true that the psalm, even when appropriated by unbelievers, provides a measure of sentimental comfort. However, in the darkest hours, genuine comfort comes only when he can confidently claim the Shepherd as his own.

It is important to remember that the concept of the shepherd is not only applied to a simple pastoral context, but also the same language is used to describe the king (II Sam. 5:2, 7:7; Jer. 3:15, 10:21, 22:22; Ezek. 34:23 and Micah 5:4). Such language was not only peculiar to Israel, but is also found among other literature of the ancient Near East. For example, King Hammurabi of Babylon called himself "the shepherd"[9] as did Abdiheba, king of Jerusalem,[10] along with Shalmaneser, Tukulti-Ninurta and Tiglath-Pileser of Assyria.[11] In Egypt, both gods and kings claimed the title of shepherd and one of the divine symbols of kingship was the shepherd's crook. The emphasis upon the shepherd qualities of a king were especially noted during the Middle Kingdom, when there was a special appeal for pharaohs to be good shepherds and lamenting when they were not.

When one understands the nature of a shepherd's responsibility, the appropriateness of that metaphor as applied to kingship is easily understood. It is clear from other psalms that the kingship of the Lord is consistently alluded to in this manner. There has been a tendency on the part of some writers to politicize rigidly the term "shepherd" and to rob many of the psalms of their more intimate associations and emphases. David, in many instances, probably did have God's kingship in mind when referring to his shepherd-sheep relationships. The metaphor, however, may be applied personally and intimately without these political or royal overtones. Unfortunately, many modern literary critics regiment such terminology into fixed categories. Whenever such a term or metaphor appears, the psalm or passage is automatically classified according to the pre-established categories. Quite often the reasoning is circular and the literature involved is robbed of its dynamic.

The shepherd motif is rich and full as measured against its ancient Near Eastern context. It provided an appropriate means of describing the ideal king, but it was also applied to other relationships as well.[13]

While the picture of the shepherd is most naturally applied to our present relationship to the Lord and His care for us as Savior, there is also a kingly or royal aspect to the term. We are not only cared for by the Great Shepherd, but we also anticipate the return of our Great King, the Chief Shepherd, who will establish His perfect kingdom.

David's final assertion in Psalm 23:1 is instructive. Literally translated he says, "I will not have need." The Hebrew verb comes from the root *ḥāsēr,* meaning to "lack, need, or be lacking." The import of this word is illustrated nicely by the language of Psalm 34:10, "The young lions *lack* and are hungry, but those seeking the Lord shall not *lack* any good thing." The Lord reminded the children of Israel that in the wilderness they "*lacked* nothing" (Deut. 2:7) and He gave them the promise that in their new land they would "not *lack* anything in it" (Deut. 8:9).

Anyone who has the Lord as his personal shepherd will never be in need. The Hebrew is emphatic at this point. But exactly what is its sense? Are we to conclude that everything a believer desires will be his? It is doubtful that one can claim this as the essence of the expression, for we are reminded in the New Testament that " . . . a man's life consisteth not in the abundance of the things which he possesseth" (Luke 12:15). What are we to say of those poor, wretched, yet godly, believers who have suffered poverty through much of their lifetimes, or of those missionaries who have experienced incredible destitution and poverty as a result of their evangelistic efforts?

No, this phrase is not a promise that anything a believer wants will be his. We are reminded by the Apostle Paul that those who live godly in Christ Jesus may well suffer persecution (II Tim. 3:12).

David is asserting that we will not lack anything that we need within the framework of God's will for our lives. In other words, there is nothing that I will lack as a child of God that will be necessary for my spiritual welfare and growth. The Good Shepherd knows precisely what His sheep need for strength and endurance, and He has provided it in abundance.

David, therefore, with the stroke of the first string in his magnificent harp, has sounded a note of provision. The rich harmony of these words continues to complement the symphonic tones of the rest of Scripture. How important it is that our ears be sensitive to its beautiful melody.

4

The Sheep

It occurred to me one day while standing in front of a college class of 125 students in Old Testament History that I should ask whether or not anyone had had direct encounter with sheep, or knew much about them. The responses were interesting and startling. Only three out of that group had ever had any amount of contact with living sheep.

One student responded, "My principal acquaintance with sheep is traced to childhood, when I was forced to master 'Little Bo Peep has lost her sheep.'" Another observation made it clear that we had some basic work to do before examining sheep and shepherd relationships in the Psalter . . . "Well, I never did know a whole lot about living sheep, but I do remember that we always got mint jelly when they served lamb chops . . . is that significant?"

I'd like to think that those freshman responses were

something less than ordinary. However, in subsequent years, I have encountered some wondrous and strange tales concerning Palestinian sheep and their nature! The views of these folk range from a very romanticized view of sheep to a very dismal appraisal of their character and capability.

More recent writers have expressed less than lofty sentiment concerning the sheep.

> It occurs to me that if Jehovah is to be our Shepherd, then we have to begin by recognizing that we are sheep. I don't like that analogy, frankly, because I don't like sheep. I come by my dislike honestly. I used to raise sheep. In high school I was in the 4-H Club, and I had a herd of sheep and goats. Goats I can abide, because they may be obnoxious, but at least they're smart. Sheep are, beyond question, the most stupid animals on the face of the earth. They are dumb and they are dirty and they are timid and defenseless and helpless. Mine were always getting lost and hurt and snakebitten. They literally do not know enough to come in out of the rain. I look back on my shepherding days with a great deal of disgust. Sheep are miserable creatures.[1]

Now if that doesn't put steam on your stained glass image of these tender little creatures, read this:

> . . . I do not doubt that it would be hard to find more stupid animals than sheep. For some reason, sheep have a remarkable aptitude for getting lost. They can be perfectly at home in a pleasant pasture, until one revolutionary spirit among them finds a hole in the fence. In less time than it takes to tell, they will desert the grass and head for the hole. In five minutes flat there won't be a sheep in the pasture and there will be hundreds on the road. Honking horns, bleating lambs, screeching tires, baaing ewes turned the quiet countryside into bedlam. All because some sheep decided to go astray, leading many others after it.[2]

While sheep will not win awards for courage, stamina or fighting ability, I doubt that they would qualify for the world's dumbest animals, although they do run a close

A flock of broad-tailed sheep, the type usually mentioned in Scripture. Levant Photo Service.

second. I once used to do a great deal of horseback riding and I think I mounted an animal that walked away with *that* award. However, sheep are mentioned more than 500 times in Scripture and that very fact should call attention to their significance.

I. Palestinian Sheep

There are nine different Hebrew terms that are variously translated, sheep, mountain sheep, ewe, lamb, and ram.[3] The most common word translated sheep or flock is *ṣōʾn*. The sheep usually mentioned in the Bible are the broadtailed type (*Ovis laticaudata*). These sheep have been so designated because of the long, broad tail that often weighs up to 25 pounds. Modern Arabs refer to the tail as *ʾalyat* or *liyat*. This is analogous to the Hebrew term *ʾālyāh* ("fat tail"). The Authorized Version translates this term with the word "rump" (Exod. 29:22; Lev. 3:9; 7:3; 8:25, and so on). After the eighth day of its life, a sheep was suitable for sacrifice (Lev.

22:19, 27) and for food (Deut. 14:4). The ram only, of this particular species, has horns; but there are other varieties of sheep in Palestine of which the ewe, also, has horns. The ram's horns were often used by priests as trumpets (Josh. 6:4) and for storing oil (I Sam. 16:1). The ram is slightly more aggressive than his spouse, but has not been remembered in natural history for his aggressive defense of either the flock or of himself. The skins of rams were dyed red and used in the construction of the tabernacle (Exod. 36:19).

II. The Character of Sheep

The Scripture reminds all of us that " . . . we like sheep have gone astray . . . ." (Isa. 53:6). That statement is not a superficial observation, but represents very accurately the disposition of sheep. While sheep are harmless, they do have a strange curiosity that causes them to wander, get lost and sometimes lose their lives in the process. Scripture many times makes allusion to this weakness (cf. Matt. 10:6; I Peter

Milking sheep. Near Deir 'Alla (Succoth). Levant Photo Service.

2:25). When sheep are without a shepherd, they are the most helpless of creatures, according to Numbers 27:17 and Matthew 9:36.

It was interestng to watch the mood and the activity of sheep in the hills of Judah. On one day in particular, I sat with Mohammad Yaseen and watched the behavior of various sheep and goats. An extended stay in this pasture area afforded me special opportunity to note the great variety of behavior patterns of sheep in particular. As I observed their change in mood and activity, I was able to discern precise parallels with members of my congregations in past years.

There were those sheep who remained with the flock and enjoyed the benefits of a selected pasture. But then there were those sometimes very young, sometimes old ewes who consistently wandered away from the flock, even though their newfound grass was of inferior quality. In fact, I found myself utterly amazed at the shabby herbage that would often attract the attention of sheep.

Then there were the belligerent rams or ewes that would predictably cause unrest in the flock. On one occasion, I sat and watched a couple of old ewes fight with each other over a small tuft of grass which they both desired. I found such a fight incredible, because all around them was an abundant supply of very tender grass and herbs. Watching them tussle brought my mind back to the indictment of James, "From whence comes wars and fightings among you? Come they not hence, even of your lusts that war in your members?" (4:1). I found it amazing that these two animals would fight over this one small portion of food when the whole pasture was theirs. I've often wondered how many of God's people are preoccupied with bitter infightings while standing knee-deep in God's richest provisions! It is with a sense of shame and disgrace that we see many undernourished Christians—not because of the Shepherd's failure to provide, but because of their preoccupation with their own selfish desires.

Some sheep were very tender and sensitive, nudging their

way to the shepherd and remaining close to him as if expecting some special favor. Other sheep, which I designated as the "explorers," were generally few in number, but insisted on moving out of the designated pasture and looking elsewhere. On one occasion, a lamb decided to select its own feeding area and found itself ultimately perched on the edge of a 500-foot cliff which we could not approach because of the fragile nature of the rock. The path leading to this place appeared secure enough, but the end of it was dangerous indeed. The writer of Proverbs stated it succinctly, "There is a way which seemeth right unto a man, but the end thereof are the ways of death" (14:12, see also 16:25).

Some sheep were very oblivious to their circumstances. These sheep would chomp away at the vegetation, oftentimes unaware of dangers around them, or even a boulder in front of them. One old ewe, in particular, constantly bumped her head or scraped her leg through this lack of circumstantial sensitivity.

Sheep provide a variety of sounds, depending on their particular circumstance. The bleating sound, however, is the most common and expected. It can be a very pitiful cry—and yet there are times when the lamb or sheep will stand silent when the danger is the greatest. I have seen a sheep stand absolutely quiet and apparently numb as the knife fell bringing about its death (Isa. 53:7). It was the bleating of the

An animal pen found on an inscriptional stone on the road between El Mefraq and Baghdad. First century B.C. From The Symbolism of the Biblical World, by Othmar Keel, Seabury Press, publishers.

sheep that produced a great embarrassment to King Saul after he failed to carry out the command of God with regard to the annihiliation of the Amalekites (I Sam. 15:14).

We would all like to think that, as believers, we are prepared to challenge and defeat all the forces 'round about us. I suspect it is a bit disconcerting to realize that, after all, we are but redeemed sheep. It is this realization that causes us to rest in the care of our Shepherd. Scripture reminds us that Satan walks about as a "roaring lion" (I Peter 5:8) and you just know that he has lamb chops on his mind! It is incumbent upon everyone of us to be close to our Shepherd, who knows the enemy and provides the defenses for His own. The danger to the flock does not always come from without, however, for we are warned that false prophets parade in sheep's clothing (Matt. 7:15). The Lord Jesus also told His own disciples that He was sending them forth " . . . as sheep in the midst of wolves: be ye therefore wise as serpents, and harmless as doves" (Matt. 10:16). This outlook is not designed to produce fear and insecurity among those who would serve Him, but is a realistic warning of the vicious hatred that they would encounter. He encouraged them with these words, "But when they deliver you up, take no thought how or what ye shall speak: for it shall be given you in that same hour what ye shall speak" (Matt. 10:19).

The lessons from the flock and the sheep are therefore inexhaustible. I have observed how well-fed sheep showed considerable strength in long journeys; but those weak and thin animals, which for a variety of reasons did not utilize the food provided, struggled in the journey. Perhaps the saddest scene of all was the bones in the desert. Time and time again while walking across the barren wilderness, I have seen the skeletal remains of a sheep or a goat that wandered off and died in the desert. This was a dramatic picture of the desperate need for leadership by the shepherd.

III. Size and Nature of the Flocks

It is often supposed that the Palestinian flock is rather

Young Arab shepherd leading his father's flock to Dothan. Levant Photo Service.

small, but this was not the case in Old Testament times, nor is it always the situation today. Job, for example, had 14,000 sheep in his flocks (cf. Job 42:12). The rich man Nabal had 3,000 sheep and 1,000 goats (cf. I Sam. 25:2). Solomon must have had vast numbers of sheep at his disposal since he was able to sacrifice 120,000 at the dedication of the temple (cf. I Kings 8:63). The Arabians are said to have brought 7,700 rams and 7,000 he-goats to Jehoshaphat for a tribute (cf. II Chron. 17:11). Such flocks would require several under-shepherds to properly count them and care for them. Normally, there were not a great number of rams in a flock. For breeding purposes, the ratio was usually no more than 1 ram to 20 ewes. Today, most of the bedouin flocks range between 30 to 75 sheep or sheep and goats. Needless to say, there are notable exceptions to this small number, but this size flock seems ideal for one shepherd to manage.

IV. The Value of the Sheep

In an agricultural-pastoral society, these animals were extremely valued and normally protected by law. Most ancient law codes and the Mosaic law made reference to the responsibilities of a shepherd and punishments for those who either stole or destroyed the animals. These animals provided food to eat, milk to drink (cf. Deut. 32:14), and wool for making cloth and covering tents. Sheep were often a medium of exchange, and commonly used for sacrifices.

Sheepshearing was usually carried out in the spring of the year and this called for a time of special celebration and festival (cf. II Sam. 13:23). The first mention of shearing is found in Genesis 31:19 in connection with Jacob's and Laban's activity. Fleeces weigh anywhere from 3 to 30 pounds, according to the particular breed and their grazing conditions.

Sheep were sometimes valuable as pets and were deeply loved by their owners. Allusion to this is made in II Samuel 12:3 when Nathan appeared before David. He spoke of a poor man who had nothing " . . . save one little ewe lamb, which he had brought and nourished up: and it grew up together with him, and with his children; it did eat of his own meat, and drank of his own cup, and lay in his bosom, and

The impression of the third millennium B.C. cylinder seal. From <u>The Symbolism of the Biblical World</u> by Othmar Keel, Seabury Press, publishers.

was unto him as a daughter."

In modern-day Palestine there are pet animals, as well. The most common of these is the *Ma³luf*. The word means "fed" or "overfed." With somewhat romantic tones, one writer describes the *Ma³luf* ram as follows:

> Its wool is short and generally black. It is a very pretty animal, having sweet hazel eyes, a nicely shaped head, and slender legs resembling those of Gilead's gazelle. Add to this an air of innocence and docility and you will not wonder that John considered it fit to be taken as an emblem of Christ. There is no comparison in beauty between our Maloof sheep and the American sheep I have seen in the Chicago stockyards. Your sheep look to me more like the Pariah dogs of Beirut and Constantinople than anything else.[5]

Often these rams were fattened for the sole purpose of providing the meat for very special festive occasions. Many of the bedouin shepherds have favorite sheep or lambs and give them special attention and care. In the household of a poor man, however, one sheep would be of the greatest value and it is in this light that Nathan challenged David. His illustration was most appropriate since David, as a shepherd, knew well the value of just one lamb. Even greater is the value of one who has been redeemed by the blood of Christ. Those who belong to the Good Shepherd are His possession.

5

Rest in His Pasture

Psalm 23:2

The oppressive heat coupled with the blowing sand made our journey through the wilderness extremely uncomfortable. Even with a well-made *keffiyeh* wrapped tightly around my head, I could feel sand in my teeth, and my eyes burned from irritation. For three hours we struggled half blindly across rocky hills and small sand dunes in an attempt to reach our destination.

Soon the roar of the winds began to subside and the only sounds that fell upon our ears were the dull thuds of footsteps and the gentle whisper of the Mediterranean breezes through small plants. When we stopped to rest, my ears caught the strains of a beautiful oriental tune being played on a reed flute. Lifting up my eyes to the horizon, I saw a sizable cluster of trees, lush grass, a small pool, along with shepherd and sheep. The mere sight of the water, along with the vegetation, began to revive my oppressed spirit. Even more invigorating was the later experience of washing my face in the cool water of that pool and relaxing in the grass with the shepherd.

Withdrawing from the clamor of a sinful world to the serenity produced by meditation in Psalm 23:2 provides the same sense of refreshment and revival of spirit. David, who penned the words of this lovely psalm, knew well what green pastures meant to the flock at the end of a long journey. But more significantly, he was well aware of the deep satisfaction one enjoyed when resting in the presence of the faithful shepherd. It was this experience that caused him to pen the following words: "In pastures of tender grass He makes me lie down and beside waters of rest He leads me." [1]

Years later, as I contemplate the imagery and richness of this passage, I can still hear the melodious strains of the shepherd's flute in the oasis. This second verse of our psalm emphasizes two important aspects of the rest provided by our Lord, the perfect Shepherd.

I. The Place of Rest

Even to the most casual observer, it is obvious that not every place is suitable for a flock of sheep to rest. Leading sheep to places where stickers or burrs are common would be both irresponsible and reckless. The wool of these animals would become matted and entangled in the plants, making shearing and wool-cleaning a frustrating task. If the shepherd is to provide adequate rest for the flock, he must also carefully avoid the carcasses of dead animals or decaying plants, which attract flies and ants. I have been amazed at the great skill bedouin shepherds exercise in locating desirable resting places. They seem to know exactly where the irritants or dangers are most likely to appear, and they judiciously avoid those places.

We should not conclude for a moment, however, that spiritual rest is achieved only by finding the most comfortable of circumstances. Such an assumption would clearly miss the mark. True rest is being where God wants the believer to be.

David described the divinely selected resting place as "pastures of fresh or tender grass" (Hebrew—*binʾôt dešeʾ*). The word *nāwâ* ("pasture") refers commonly to the abode of the shepherd or his flocks. It is applied to the resting place of sheep (II Sam. 7:8; I Chron. 17:17 and Isa. 65:10) and of camels (Ezek. 25:5). The term is also widely used in the Old Testament for habitations, usually of a country or domains within a country.[2]

The original word for grass (Hebrew—*dešeʾ*) is enlightening because it often refers to fresh, new grass (Deut. 32:2; II Sam. 23:4 and Prov. 27:25). The place of rest David described, therefore, was a rich, lush pastureland with an abundance of tender green grass. While the land of Palestine and Transjordan had its vast grazing areas, the number of places that could be described with the above terms were few in number. During the winter and early spring rains, there would be many hills covered with vegetation, but the blistering summer sun would soon quickly destroy that beauty. The only green pasture areas that would remain would be those near streams, rivers or springs. It is quite startling to travel through vast stretches of desert and then come upon an oasis with its water surrounded by thick vegetation.

It might be observed at this point that settlement patterns in Palestine were often affected by the presence or absence of permanent water supplies. The great cities of the Old Testament were able to exist for centuries, largely because of the presence of dependable water sources. There were other factors, of course, that influenced settlement patterns, but water was certainly one of the key reasons for the growth and continued existence of a major city.

There are a number of pasturelands mentioned in the Bible which give some indication of their importance. Micah and Isaiah both refer to the "sheep of Bozrah" (Micah 2:12; Isa. 34:6). Grazing areas were found in Bashan and Gilead (Micah 7:14), Arabia (Isa. 60:7) and Judah. It will be remembered that David cared for his father's flocks in the vicinity of

Bethlehem (I Sam. 16:4, 11). It was also near Bethlehem that shepherds were caring for their flocks when the announcement of Jesus' birth was made (Luke 2:8-20). The very presence of sheep and shepherds in the hill country would suggest that those events took place not in winter, but probably in the spring.

Pastures provide a place for both feeding and resting. Surely this is what David had in mind when he spoke of the Lord's leadership and the rest that He provided. It is God's perfect leading that makes rest and refreshment possible.

Our culture has been greatly blessed both in *meal* as well as in *mercy*. We have a general abundance of food for the body and are certainly overwhelmed with the potential for spiritual enrichment through modern communications and the printed page. The fact that we are so greatly blessed puts a serious obligation upon every believer for consistent spiritual growth and effective service. Surely God will hold all Christians accountable for the tremendous amount of light which is available to us in these days.

Unfortunately, in spite of the spiritual heritage that we have, there is still a vast number of Christians who are undernourished and anemic. Even though they live in pastures with great potential, they refuse to feed and are preoccupied with other activities. What a tragedy that we should be in the midst of such great provision and still continue to suffer spiritual malnutrition.

One writer has suggested that the pasture referred to in this verse is actually a synonym for "the house of the Lord."[3] While it is true that the term for pastures is often applied to dwelling places, it is doubtful that is the sense of the word here.

The place of rest to which the Lord leads His own is not only characterized by the presence of green grass, but cool, fresh water. It is unfortunate that the Hebrew expression *mê mᵉnuḥôṯ* is translated "still waters" in the Authorized Version, because the word *mᵉnuḥôṯ* is not an attribute of the waters. Alexander observes: "By waters of rest we are not to

"He makes me lie down in green pastures." Matson Photo Service

understand still or quiet waters, a sense which the Hebrew word has nowhere else, and which would here suggest the idea of stagnation, or at least that of silence, which is far less agreeable that that of an audible flow. The idea really conveyed is that of waters, by or at which rest may be enjoyed."[4] Isaiah's use of this word helps to reinforce this observation: "And my people shall dwell in a peaceable habitation, and in sure dwellings, and in quiet *resting places*" (Hebrew—*ûḇimnûḥōṯ šaᵃnannôṯ,* Isa. 32:18).

The "still waters" of the Authorized Version has led a number of writers to erroneous generalizations about the drinking habits of sheep. For example we are told: "sheep are afraid of running water; they will drink only from a quiet pool."[5] Another asserts: "sheep are very timid; they are afraid of swift water, and will drink only of still water."[6] While it is true sheep are not likely to step into a rushing stream or treacherous river, they nonetheless do drink from slow-moving brooks and streams, even with the presence of rocks. On numerous occasions, I have watched sheep drinking at ᶜEin Farah and they seemed undisturbed by the moving water.

Of course sheep are normally very reticent to approach rushing water where there are many large rocks. On one occasion, Abas Tawfeek approached a gushing stream of water coming through a small wadi shortly after a spring rain. He observed the fact that the water was very muddy and unattractive to the sheep, so he gathered large rocks and put them across the stream, slowing the movement of the water. As the water backed up and its movement slowed down, the sediment filtered to the bottom and the sheep drank freely. But even in this situation, the water continued to move at a considerable pace.

I can remember well the refreshment of both soul and spirit at being able to drink cool water and lie down in the grass after an arduous journey through the wilderness. My spirit was lifted and my endurance renewed. I rather suspect that the believer who is led by the Lord through the wilderness of

"He leads me beside still waters." Matson Photo Service.

this world enjoys equal refreshment as he finds himself in the Lord's pastures, rich in green grass, and plenteous in fresh water.

The Oriental shepherd actually had several kinds of water supplies at his disposal. There were the few rivers that flow in Palestine, the most popular of which is the Jordan. In some places, there are pools that are fed by underground springs. It is this type of water supply that supports the beautiful oases in the desert.

Water was commonly made available to sheep and goats from the many cisterns that were dug in the hillsides and deserts. These are usually pear-shaped cuts in the rock which have a stone across the small opening to prevent accidents (Exod. 21:33-34). It was not uncommon for the Israelites to plaster the insides of such cisterns with lime to reduce the porosity of the walls. Both Joseph (Gen. 37:22) and Jeremiah (Jer. 38:6) were cast into such pits. In modern-day Jordan, not just anyone can use the water from these storage places. There are usually agreements established between villagers and the shepherds as to who may use the water of the cisterns and how often.

The Hebrew words *bôr* or *bō'r*, both of which come from the verb *bā'ar* ("to dig") refer to subterranean chambers. This term is used to describe cisterns, but also cylindrical wells ($b^e{}'\bar{e}r$) which receive water through their walls. The tremendous importance of such wells is illustrated by Isaac's conflicts with the Philistines of Gerar. He re-dug many of the wells which Abraham had utilized earlier, only to incur resistance from herdsmen living in Gerar (Gen. 26:14-22). Battles over watering holes in wilderness areas continue even to this day among some desert-dwelling peoples.

II. The Pattern of Rest

Not only does the Lord lead us to appropriate pastures for our spiritual good, but it is He who actually makes rest in such pastures possible. The Hebrew verb *yarbîṣēnî* suggests a causal sense. It is derived from the root *rābaṣ* which means "to stretch, lie out, or recline." How does He accomplish this?—simply by removing our fears and enabling us to rest in His presence. This rest and refreshment is not intended to be an end in itself. The Lord leads us to pastures so we may grow and gain strength for continued journey and service. Believers are not encouraged to enter His rest merely for the personal comfort or satisfaction it provides, although these are promised benefits.

The Lord gave the Israelites a promise of a homeland, and they were expected to conquer that land—and in so doing would be "entering into His rest" (Heb. 4:1-11). The writer of Hebrews emphasized the fact that true spiritual rest is in essence the abandonment of carnal works and a complete reliance upon the Lord (Heb. 4:9-11).

Many Christians operate under the false assumption that mere church activity is, in itself, the key to spiritual growth. While such activity might contribute to the maturing process in a Christian, it is no substitute for personal study in the Word of God and the appropriation of that truth. Far too often religious activity is carnally inspired. One is reminded of Jeremiah's indictment of ancient Israel, "For my people have committed two evils; they have forsaken me the fountain of living waters, and hewed them out cisterns, broken cisterns, that can hold no water" (Jer. 2:13). Needless to say, there is nothing more useless in Palestine than a broken or cracked cistern. Furthermore, what shepherd would prefer the water of a cistern above that of a free-flowing spring or stream?

It is tragic indeed to wander through the rich pastures provided by the Lord and see Christians still anemic and spiritually inept. The fault, of course, is not in the quality of the pasture, but in the sheep who fail to feed there. They are not ignorant of feeding techniques. In fact, they have become spiritual recipe collectors; they know all the formulas for enriching growth, but they have never appropriated the actual food for themselves.

In contrast to those sheep who do not eat in spite of the Lord's provision, there are those who are spiritually corpulent as the result of overfeeding and inactivity. Their muscles are never exercised in journeys across rugged hillsides to touch the hearts of others with the Gospel of Christ. Their faith, with all of its joy, is hoarded instead of being shared. It is distressing to see the sleeping cars of the gospel train jammed full, while the engine room is begging for committed laborers.

It was getting near sunset as Mohammad Yaseen and I made our way toward the small brook which had an abundance of herbage on either side. We approached a large pool which certainly would have been suitable to quench the thirst of the sheep, which had been on the move for several hours. The flock, however, refused to approach the pool for one simple reason. On the other side was a large dog that had wandered down from a nearby village. This situation made it clear that the mere presence of water and pasture would not guarantee rest and refreshment for the flock. There had to be safety and security.

There are a number of things which prevent the sheep from enjoying complete rest—and the presence of fear is one of them. Mohammad reached into the leather pouch that was on his side and removed a sling made of twisted cord with a leather pouch in the center. He selected a sizable stone and began to whirl the sling over his head and ultimately released the stone in the direction of the dog. The stone struck the ground with an impressive thud and the dog ran in the opposite direction. Mohammad then went down to the waters and stood by the edge, indicating complete safety. Sure enough, little by little, the sheep made their way to the water's edge and drank in peace. I was reminded of Jesus' words recorded in Luke 12:32: "Fear not, little flock, for it is your Father's good pleasure to give you the kingdom." The Psalmist also encouraged us to "Rest in the Lord, and wait patiently for him . . ." (Ps. 37:7).

I was fascinated by the fact that even after the dog had fled,

"He restoreth my soul." Courtesy Matson Photo Service.

the sheep did not move toward the water until Mohammad stood at its edge for several minutes. It reminded me that it is the presence of the shepherd that gives real security, not just the absence of a dog.

Another factor which prevents a flock of sheep from enjoying rest is extreme hunger. Such sheep will continue to wander about restlessly, looking for food to satisfy that hunger.

A flock of sheep or goats might also be denied rest by constant belligerency among its members. Time and time again we witnessed battles between members of a flock of sheep and goats which created an uneasiness among the others; so much so that they refused to lie down and rest. Surely our Lord is saddened when He looks upon the rich pastures He has provided only to see His own sheep fighting among themselves—and usually over the most insignificant of matters. Their preoccupation with selfish interest has prevented them from touching the lives of those who desperately need the Gospel. Organizations within the church are often divided and compete with one another, rather than complementing the ministry of the pastor. One has well said that when Lucifer was cast out of heaven, he landed in the choir loft! Equally distressing is the fact that many Christians are weary and worn—not because of intensive conflict with the evil one, but because of petty arguments among themselves (1 Cor. 1:10-12 and James 4:1-3).

The pattern of rest is also reflected in the verb employed by David in the second clause of our verse. He simply stated that the Lord leads us beside waters of rest, or waters by which rest may be enjoyed. The Hebrew verb *nāhal* suggests the idea of gentle guidance. Isaiah used the word in this manner: "He shall feed his flock like a shepherd: he shall gather the lambs with his arm, and carry them in his bosom, and shall *gently lead* those that are with young" (Isa. 40:11). That same tender, sensitive leading is reflected also in Isaiah 49:10: "They shall not hunger nor thirst; neither shall the heat nor sun smite them: for he that hath mercy on them shall *lead* them, even by the springs of water shall he guide them." (See also: Isa. 51:18; Ps. 77:20 and John 10:4.)

The prospects for believers who, like sheep, follow the shepherd closely include protection in the journey and great refreshment in pastures of rest. The strengthening of the body and the reviving of the soul comes when the believer reaches those pastures, and through thirst and hunger of soul, eats and drinks that which is necessary for growth. Jesus said: "Blessed are they which do hunger and thirst after righteousness: for they shall be filled" (Matt. 5:6).

6

Restoration and Restraint

Psalm 23:3

Among the necessary qualities of a good shepherd is his ability to provide whatever is necessary to restore the weary, weak sheep. An extended journey is not even possible, unless along the way the sheep are properly fed and rested.

The safety of the flock's movement is equally important. There is no merit in feeding a flock of sheep only to have them destroyed by wandering along the wrong path. In the third verse of this delightful psalm, David reminded us that our journey takes its toll and we all are in need of refreshment and uplifting of soul and spirit. Because we are sheep we also need the disciplined guidance of the perfect Shepherd.

I. Restoration of the Sheep

It is not accidental that David should point to restoration following the blessings of the pasturelands recorded in verse

2. The expected and natural result of rest, as provided by the Lord, is the revival of the weary soul.

The Hebrew word translated "soul" (*nepes̆*) in this passage is often employed in the Old Testament to describe the whole man. It is frequently translated by the word "life." But here, as in Psalm 19:7, the reference seems to be to the vivifying or quickening of the exhausted spirit.[1]

Needless to say, sheep which travel long distances through rugged terrain soon feel the effects of exhaustion. What is true of sheep physically is certainly true of the child of God spiritually. Those who follow the Lord closely in those narrow paths of righteousness and engage in the rigors of service will soon find spirit and soul exhausted and in want of restoration. It is for this reason that it is mandatory for every believer to return to the Word of God constantly for restoration of soul and refreshment of spirit. This was illustrated to me on one of my field trips in the wilderness of Judah.

We began our journey on a chilly Saturday morning south of Tekoa. By ten o'clock the heat had already become oppressive and our water supply was exhausted. Not having a sufficient supply of fresh water was a mistake, but not fatally so. As I approached an open area, I could see a large bedouin encampment with one magnificent tent standing out above the others. I was met by an elderly gentleman who spoke with a deep voice, "*marḥabā*" ("Hello"). I returned the greeting in Arabic and soon after we were joined by his son who spoke very fluent English. As is the case among bedouin Arabs, hospitality is very much a way of life. It is not something to be endured, but an honor carefully sought after. By the time I reached the tent, every muscle in my body ached with exhaustion and even my mind was clouded because of the oppressiveness of the long journey.

After some conversation and a few cups of hot Turkish coffee, I was given a delightful meal prepared by the man's wife. The food was prepared in another sector of the tent where the ladies had gathered. The tent was divided by a cloth

Bedouin tents in the Judean wilderness. Levant Photo Service.

The author discusses shepherding with young Arabs in Jordan. Photo by the author.

that went across the center, and instructions were given by the elderly gentleman through that partition. Not until the food was ready to be served did his wife appear. As I sat on the small rug preparing to eat, my mind was drawn back to the events of Genesis 18 and once again I remembered that the Orient and its customs change very slowly.

After an hour or two of rest after the meal, I found myself completely refreshed and even startled by the fact I was speaking enthusiastically about an additional journey that day. Two hours before, I had real doubts as to whether I could continue another five feet. It was amazing what food, water and rest did for both body and soul.

I have experienced the same refreshment when coming to the Word of God hungry and weary, only to find that the Lord's provisions were more than adequate for the needs of my soul. What a tragedy that we often struggle in the journey and groan out of exhaustion when God has made more than ample provision for our needs.

Some commentators have handled the concept of

restoration in Psalm 23:3 as a disciplinary act on the part of the shepherd.

> One day the shepherd comes over the hilltop and instead of gently and patiently leading the wayward sheep back to the flock, he reaches down and takes one of the slender front legs in his hand and strikes it a sudden blow with the shepherd's crook and there is a sheep with a broken leg. Broken by the shepherd! He then prepares splints and binds up the broken leg. Thereafter, the wounded sheep must of necessity keep close to the shepherd for he must carry it over rough spots and across the mountain streams. But the point is, the shepherd has restored the sheep.[2]

This interpretation of the first clause of this verse is most strange, indeed, and seems to miss the mark at two points. First, the emphasis is not on discipline, especially of a type that would incapacitate the animal so as to make it burdensome to the shepherd. Second, it is inconceivable that the shepherd would mar a sheep in this manner, especially if he were tending the flocks of another. I have seen shepherds poke and beat sheep with their rod, but never to a point that would break bones and require the splinting described in the above paragraph. This is not to say that the shepherd does not exercise discipline. He does indeed, and that is reflected in the second clause of our verse; but it is very doubtful that the activity suggested above is in any way typical of a real shepherd.

II. Restraint of the Sheep

Not only does a good shepherd provide all that is necessary so that his sheep may regain strength and be properly prepared for subsequent journey, but he makes it a point to guide the sheep in such a way that the destination will be reached with safety. David stated it this way, "He will lead me in paths of righteousness, for the sake of His name."[3]

The Hebrew word translated "lead" (*nāḥâ*) here is different from the word rendered "lead" in verse 2 (where it is *nāhal*).

The term here is stronger and more definitive. It is commonly used of God's leadership of His people Israel (Gen. 13:17; 15:13 and Isa. 58:11). This term is also used with respect to guiding a flock as in Psalm 77:20, "Thou *leddest* thy people like a flock by the hand of Moses and Aaron."

According to David, the Lord guides or leads us in "tracks or entrenchments" of righteousness. The noun *ma^{c}gāl* can be used of an entrenchment (I Sam. 17:20 and 26:5) or the tracks made by the frequent use of wagons. One would assume from such usage that its metaphorical application would refer to those paths or tracks which are clearly defined and safe; or, in the case of this verse, those tracks or paths which are morally correct.

There have been some who have suggested that the reference here is to "straight paths," that is, flat, smooth areas as opposed to rugged places. But surely this misses the mark. David is not promising that the Lord will lead us only through the smooth places. In fact, we are clearly reminded by the Apostle Paul that "all who live godly in Christ Jesus will suffer persecution" (II Tim. 3:12). The use of this noun metaphorically for the way or course of life is common in the Old Testament (Prov. 4:26), and it is frequently applied to the good or right manner of life. The writer of Proverbs stated: "I have taught thee in the way of wisdom; I have led thee in right paths" (Prov. 4:11, see also 2:9 and Isa. 26:7). Of course it was used to designate an evil way of life as well (Prov. 2:15, 18; 5:6 and Isa. 59:8).

Because of the inherent weaknesses of sheep, it is essential that the shepherd provide complete leadership. Sheep are just not capable of distinguishing between trails that lead to safety and those that will end in danger or death.

The silence of the hillside was broken in a frightening manner as Abas Tawfeek and I heard the pitiful cries of a young goat. We rushed to the edge, only to see that the small goat had wandered down what looked like a perfectly stable path and was now perched on a rock so small it could not even turn around. Abas fortunately was well prepared for contingencies just like that, and retrieved a long piece of rope from his pouch. He made a noose at the one end of the rope, opened it, dropped it down to the cliff, slipped it over the neck of the goat and quickly pulled him off the ledge.

I have recalled that event many times since then and each time I have been reminded of two important features. First is the lack of the animal's ability to discern danger from safety in a trail. What appeared to be a perfectly safe path to travel could easily have led to the death of that goat. It had very limited vision and could not see around the curve where the small trail ended. We, like sheep and goats, also have low visibility and desperately need guidance of an omnipresent, omniscient Lord.

The second thing that struck me on that occasion was the incredible patience of Abas Tawfeek. That was the fourth time he had to retrieve that little goat! For some reason it insisted on wandering into difficult and dangerous places. I suppose that, for many of us, patience would have lasted only beyond the second time before we would have clobbered the goat in a fit of anger for its recalcitrant attitude.

On this fourth occasion, I turned to Abas and said, "How is it you have such great patience with this animal? You disciplined it each time, and yet it continues to wander." His response to my question was brief and enlightening. "It is only an animal," he said, "only a small goat." Perhaps our praise ought to be that of the psalmist, who declared: "But thou, O Lord, art a God full of compassion, and gracious, longsuffering, and plenteous in mercy and truth" (Ps. 86:15).

I think I detect that same tender patience in Luke 15:4-5 when the Lord spoke the parable of the lost sheep to the Pharisees. A wealthy man may have had 100 sheep, but if one was lost, that was considered a serious loss, even if it was a stubborn little animal.

As I watched Abas walk across the hill with that little goat in his arms, I could not help but be reminded of the well-known parable of the prodigal son. Having wasted many days of his life in riotous living, he returned home in repentance—hurt, wounded and in despair. He cried out that he was no longer worthy to be called a son (Luke 15:19); but when he came to his father, there was rejoicing. And the father instructed his servants: "Bring forth the best robe, and put it on him; put a ring on his hand, and shoes on his feet: and bring hither the fatted calf, and kill it; and let us eat, and be merry: for this my son was dead, and is alive again; he was lost, and is found" (Luke 15:22-24). I was impressed with the joy and satisfaction easily discernible on the face of Abas Tawfeek. How much more must the face of this father have shown joy when his wandering son returned. But even greater is the joy of the Father, our Shepherd, who witnesses the return of one of His own to the flock.

The lessons from this incident are manifold. First, we are able to learn something of the value of just one sheep or goat. A superficial assessment may bring the conclusion that one animal is easily expendable if the flock is large. But in the shepherd's sight, each animal is precious.

There is a second impression that one gains from the experience of the little goat. Among the virtues absolutely necessary for the good shepherd is patience.

I cannot leave these thoughts without considering the application of these truths to the Christian pastor. Woe be to that man who assumes that his charm and intellectual sophistication will guarantee that every member of the flock will follow him without incident. He should also be reminded that young people, like young lambs, tend to wander and get into difficulty. It is in the nature of both. Therefore, with tender patience and appropriate discipline, one leads, guides and exhorts. To do otherwise is only to guarantee failure in the gospel ministry and to experience extreme personal frustration.

Of course it goes without saying that lambs well fed and disciplined may be expected to grow into strong sheep which will not normally wander and jeopardize themselves through immature decisions. The leadership of a pastor should be consistent and in paths of righteousness.

I remember vividly sitting on the west side of the ancient mound of Tekoa after a difficult morning of excavation in an Iron Age tomb. The warm, soft breeze coming from the Mediterranean to the west made this a delightful and refreshing experience. While gazing across the valley, I was able to see a young bedouin shepherd with a very large flock of sheep. He was a bit careless as he walked beside the sheep down the trail and was throwing rocks at various objects, not aware of the fact that there was a fork in the trail to the south. The result was that when the flock reached the fork, some sheep went to the southeast and others went to the southwest. The sheep had no way of knowing which direction, for both trails looked quite inviting and adequate. It was his responsibility, of course, to have anticipated this difficulty and to move to the front of the flock in order to provide guidance.

Not more than 20 minutes later, another smaller flock of sheep and goats came up the trail, but this time with an elderly shepherd walking directly in front of them. He approached the same fork in the trail, moved to the left with every member of the flock right behind him; no problems, no division, no confusion. The difference was in the

Shepherds with sheep in the fields of Bethlehem. Levant Photo Service.

leadership. David rejoiced in the fact that he was led in paths of righteousness by his Shepherd.

But what is the reason for all of this? Is there something in the sheep that compels the shepherd to guide them and provide for them? The psalmist made it clear that whatever the Lord does, he does by His grace; or, to use the Hebrew idea, "for the sake of His name." The reason for God's acts is not found in the merits of human effort, nor in the need or desire for profit, but in and because of Himself.

Whenever the word "name" is used, it alludes not just to the identifying title of the Lord, but to His very nature. This is no better illustrated than in the classic response to Moses' inquiry concerning the name of his God: "And God said unto Moses, I AM THAT I AM: and he said, Thus shalt thou say unto the children of Israel, I AM has sent me unto you" (Exod. 3:14). The name of the Lord was important. Notice, for example, the deep concern of Joshua after Israel's initial defeat at Ai. Joshua cried out in prayer, " . . . what wilt thou do unto thy great name?" (Joshua 7:9). The Lord's covenant faithfulness was at stake here, and Joshua was fearful that both Israel and her enemies would lose respect for that name. Of course it was not the failure of the Lord that brought about the dismal performance of Israel at Ai, but sin within the camp. Once that had been cared for, victory belonged to God's people.

We need to be reminded that, as sinners, the only thing God is obligated to do is to judge us in the light of His perfect holiness. Whatever we have in salvation and subsequent blessing is due solely to His grace and mercy. His mercy withholds the very thing that we do deserve—namely, judgment. His grace, on the other hand, provides the very thing we do not deserve; that is, salvation through His blood. There is nothing within ourselves that merits this kind of love. The impact of this truth is humbling. But then again we should be reminded that, after all, we are only sheep that have been redeemed by a gracious God.

With David, we are able to rejoice that in the spiritual

barrenness of this present age, He is able to restore our weary souls; and in the complexity of life, He is able to lead us in paths of righteousness. The purpose of all of this is not merely to provide comfort for the sheep, but to bring glory to the Shepherd. The delightful chorus written by Sidney Cox captures the spirit of Psalm 23:2: "My Lord knows the way through the wilderness, all I have to do is follow."

7

Protection for
the Journey

Psalm 23:4

"You may take the flock yourself today, my son, but guard them ... guard them well."

These words, so heavy with responsibility, were spoken to 15-year-old Abdul who was about to take his father's flock to the grazing areas for the first time.

Abdul's response, in Arabic, was both moving and meaningful to me. Literally translated, he said, "I will guard them to the best of my strength ... my life for theirs."

It is possible that nearly 3,000 years ago David, the young son of Jesse, uttered very similar words as he prepared to take his father's flocks into the hills surrounding Bethlehem. He was but a teenager at the time (Hebrew na^{c}ar, see I Sam. 17:33).

David encountered some rather hair-raising experiences in defense of his father's flock. When he stood before Saul, prior to his encounter with the Philistine giant, Goliath, he described his experiences in the following words, ". . . Thy servant kept his father's sheep, and there came a lion, and a bear, and took a lamb out of the flock: and I went out after him, and smote him, and delivered it out of his mouth: and when he arose against me, I caught him by his beard, and smote him, and slew him. Thy servant slew both the lion and the bear. . . ." (I Sam. 17:34-36).

History records numerous incidents of shepherds encountering wild animals and thieves, and having to surrender their lives in defense of the flock. The one difference between these stories and the promises given by the Great Shepherd is that our Lord cannot be overwhelmed by any enemy. That is why David, in this soul-strengthening verse, was able to find comfort even though he knew well that there were many dangers ahead.

The Lord Jesus not only declared His love for the sheep, but, as a Good Shepherd, gave His life for the sheep (John 10:11). This act was a clear indication that He was the true Shepherd in contrast to the hireling who, when seeing a wild animal, would often leave the sheep and allow them to be scattered. The explanation for this, according to John 10:13, is that he "cared not for the sheep."

I. Crisis in the Journey

Verse 4 of this Shepherd Psalm begins with two interesting little words in the Hebrew text (*gam kî*). These words literally translated would be "even though." David is pointing out that the Lord's protection and guidance is easily assumed when we are by "waters of rest." But now he is emphasizing the fact that we may rejoice in the Lord's leadership and protection "even though" our journey takes us through the darkest experience.

It is fashionable these days to propose rather superficial responses to difficult circumstances or experiences. One evangelist was engaged in very emotional appeals to a large congregation to forget the troubles of the world and, when difficulties and frustrations occur, to merely smile and shout

"Praise the Lord." That all sounded rather impressive until this writer saw him in action. As we rode in his new car through a torrential rainstorm, he got a flat tire. Needless to say, his mood and conversation failed to reflect his earlier admonitions as he stood dripping in the rain removing the lug bolts!

David had this to say about the nature of our crisis, "Even though I should walk in the valley of extreme dangers I will not be afraid."[1] But what exactly does David mean by "shadow of death"? The Hebrew word employed in this verse has been variously explained. Some feel that it is a compound of two words ṣēl ("shadow") and môṭ ("death"). Both the Septuagint and the Targums have taken "shadow of death" as composed of these two words. Many commentators, however, reject this identification, stating that ". . . the Hebrew almost never forms compound nouns except in the case of proper names."[2] Delitzsch, following this line of argument, suggested that the word was formed from the verb ṣlm meaning "to overshadow, or darken."[3]

In a recent article by D. W. Thomas, the suggestion is made that the word "death" is used here to provide a superlative force to "shadow," thus indicating a "very deep/thick darkness."[4] Mitchell Dahood agrees with this assessment: ". . . The vocalization of ṣalmāweṭ may prove to be correct, with māweṭ serving the function of a superlative. Composite nouns in Hebrew are more frequent than grammars allow, especially since thay are clearly attested in the Ras Shamra tablets. . . ."[5]

Whether one derives the form from the verbal root ṣlm meaning "to overshadow," or a compound Hebrew word made up of ṣēl and môṭ ("death shadow"), the sense appears to be generally the same. The writer is not merely referring to death, but ". . . to all dark and bitter experiences, one of which may be death."[6]

The use of the word in other Old Testament contexts would seem to support this idea. For example, Jeremiah had this to say, "Neither said they, Where is the LORD that

"Even though I walk through the valley of the shadow of death, I will fear no evil
. . . thy rod and thy staff they comfort me." Matson Photo Service.

brought us up out of the land of Egypt, that led us through the wilderness, through a land of deserts and of pits, through a land of drought, and of the *shadow of death* through a land that no man passed through, and where no man dwelt?" (Jer. 2:6). The sense of the expression here is a blend of imminent danger and possible death. A similar use is found in Psalm 44:19.

One must remember that the hill country of Judah is broken up by narrow and precipitous ravines or wadis through which one must go in order to get to the flatlands of the Jordan Valley or the Dead Sea. They abound with caves which provide perfect hiding places for both wild beasts and robbers. One speaker made light of these dark experiences by pointing out to his congregation that "only fools and children are afraid of shadows. After all, the shadow of a sword can't cut and the shadow of a dog won't bite." I had to smile as I heard this shallow philosophical approach to the realities of life. These words were uttered by one who apparently had not walked in the valleys through which shepherds and sheep must go. Furthermore, where there is a shadow, there is a reality. If I should see the shadow of a large dog with its bare teeth coming toward me, I would not remain still merely because I could not see the dog itself. Common sense would tell me that shadow is being produced by something and my suspicion would be it was an actual dog.

It is dangerous for a believer to make light of the dangers and the deceptions that the evil one can provide. Satan, that roaring lion who walks about seeking whom he might devour, is a deadly enemy. I remember well the following limerick which serves as a warning to all.

A smiling young man from Niger
Rode on the back of a tiger;
At the end of the ride,
He was on the inside,
And the smile was on the face of the tiger!

But David did not speak of the valley of the death shadow

to strike fear into the heart of the sheep, but to remind them that their safety is found in the Shepherd. God never promised immunity from sorrow, but He did offer the grace to endure and overcome it. It is wrong to dwell on the dangers of the valley without considering the strength of the Shepherd. Too many Christians are overwhelmed with a spiritual pessimism because they dwell only on the evil of this world and quickly forget the great power of the Good Shepherd.

David knew by experience the tragedies of this life, but he was also able to face them without fear.

II. Comfort in Jehovah

The grand testimony of David in the light of potential danger was "I will not fear evil (danger) because you are with me." Notice carefully he did not say "I will encounter no evil." Such a statement would have been contrary to his own experience, as well as the teaching of Scripture.

We need to be reminded of the fact that fear is one of the great enemies of a flock of sheep. When there is sudden fear, the sheep are scattered and often this results in injury and death. David did not derive comfort from the weakness of the enemy or his inherent strength, but from the fact that the Lord was with him. When one fully understands the import of the doctrine of God's omnipotence and omnipresence, there is always a sense of confidence and comfort. These lofty truths are not included in the Psalter to merely round out theological viewpoints. They are there, and elsewhere in Scripture, to strengthen the faith of those who follow the Lord and bring comfort in His service.

While excavating ancient tombs at biblical Heshbon, I had opportunity to observe a large dark cave at the bottom of a wadi. I had earlier entered the cave with a large stick and had probed its corners for snakes and scorpions and checked the ceiling for any damage due to earthquake. As far as I could determine, the cave was perfectly safe for entrance. Little

Mohammad, from a nearby village, had come to watch our work and I took him to my side and invited him into the cave. He refused to enter, noting the darkness before him and the uncertainty of that situation. I continued to encourage him and reminded him that I had already been in the cave and no danger was present. I even flexed my muscles to show him that I could protect him, but this did not change his attitude. (Upon later reflections in the mirror, I think I can understand why this was not a particularly effective tactic!) Moments later, Mohammad's father came along to view our work as well. He looked at the cave and said to Mohammad, "Let's go inside and examine the work." To my utter amazement, Mohammad took his father's hand and walked into the cave without blinking an eye! I asked Mohammad why he had changed his mind and he simply answered, "My father is here. I am not afraid to enter the cave."

This is precisely the sentiment of Psalm 23. David was able to assert confidently that he would not fear, simply because the Lord, his Shepherd, was always with him. The presence of the Lord has provided encouragement for saints throughout the ages. When Jacob was at Bethel, the Lord promised, ". . . I am with thee, and will keep thee in all places whither thou goest, and will bring thee again into this land; for I will not leave thee, until I have done that which I have spoken to thee of" (Gen. 28:15). As Joshua stood on the east bank of the Jordan river, ready to lead that great throng of Israelites into Canaan, the Lord strengthened him with these words, "There shall not any man be able to stand before thee all the days of thy life: as I was with Moses, so I will be with thee: I will not fail thee, nor forsake thee" (Joshua 1:5). When Jesus commissioned His disciples to carry the Gospel to all nations, baptizing them in the name of the Father and of the Son and of the Holy Spirit, He encouraged them with the words, "I am with you alway, even unto the end of the world" (Matt. 28:20).

After asserting the reason for his comfort, David added this statement, "thy rod and thy staff they comfort me." Two

A Bedouin shepherd with his rod. Levant Photo Service.

questions arise here. First, what were the rod and the staff to which he alluded; and second, in what way could they possibly bring comfort? Even though two different Hebrew words are used here to describe the implements, there are some who suggest that only one object was actually in view. It is their assertion that the one implement had two functions.

But the use of these Hebrew words and our knowledge of oriental shepherding would seem to point to two distinct implements. The word translated "rod" (Hebrew—*šebeṭ*) may designate not only the shepherd's rod (Lev. 27:32) but a teacher's staff (II Sam. 7:14; Prov. 13:24), a ruler's scepter (Gen. 49:10; Isa. 14:5) and a weapon (II Sam. 23:21).

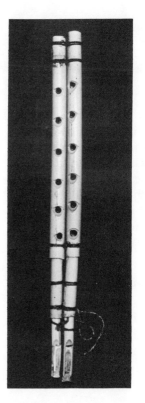

The shepherd's flute and sling. Flute: photo by Art Davis. Sling: Courtesy Andrews University Archaeological Museum. Photographed by Eugenia Nitowski.

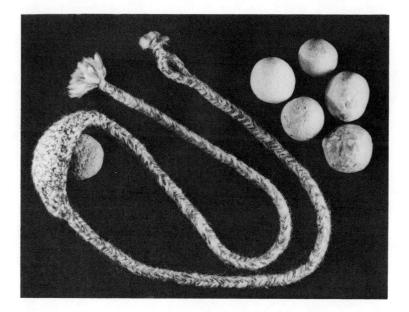

George M. Mackie describes this rod in the following manner:

> Hanging by his side, or sheathed in a long narrow pouch attached to his cloak, is his oak club. It is carefully chosen, a straight young tree being often torn up for this purpose, and the bulb at the beginning of the root being trimmed to make the head of the club. The handle is dressed to the required thickness with a hole at the end by which it is tied to the belt, or hangs from the wrist like a riding whip. It is the "rod" of Psalm 23:4. It appears in Assyrian sculpture, as the emblem of power in the hand of the king, and was the original of the scepter, mace and baton.[8]

The word translated "staff" is *mišᶜenet* which is generally considered to be a longer stick, up to six feet in length. It serves as an aid in climbing over rocks, in chastising loitering sheep and fighting goats; and the elderly are able to use it for a support (Exod. 21:19 and Zech. 8:4). I was interested to note that Mohammad Yaseen used his staff to check the crevices in caves in order to chase out snakes or scorpions that might endanger himself or his flock.

It might be profitable to pause here and examine the other equipment carried by the Palestinian shepherd. One of the popular weapons carried by shepherds in antiquity, and by modern-day bedouins as well, is the sling. We have already alluded to David's use of the sling (Hebrew—*qelaᶜ*) which was used to ward off wild beasts and to prevent sheep from straying. It was a popular weapon among the Benjamites, whose skill was recognized by the writer of Judges: "Among all this people there were seven hundred chosen men lefthanded; every one could sling stones at an hair breadth, and not miss" (Judges 20:16). It is of special interest that the 1974 expedition at Raddanna discovered numerous quantities of stones dating to the end of the twelfth century B.C. This site is located in Benjamite territory and may well have suffered destruction in the Benjamite conflict recorded in Judges 20 (I Chron. 12:2). The sling was made of either leather or goathair. If leather, it could be plaited or consist of a single strip, and was broadened in the middle to form a pocket for the stone. When goathair was utilized, the two strings had strands of white and black interwoven with one of them, at least, having an opening at the end for the fingers. Both ends were held firmly in the hand as the sling was whirled over the head, till one end was suddenly released.

The shepherd also had a small bag, or scrip, which hung at his side (I Sam. 17:40) into which he was able to put bread, olives, cheese, raisins and dried figs. David used this bag to carry the stones needed for his sling.

The shepherd also wore a large cloak, which could be utilized as a blanket in the cool evenings. Musical instruments, especially the double-reed flute, were common

A young shepherd with a sling. Matson Photo Service.

among ancient oriental shepherds and are still utilized today. A shepherd may also make use of the services of one or more dogs to help safeguard a large flock (Job 30:1). It is not uncommon to see modern shepherds with a rifle or pistol for protection.

But how then do "the rod and staff" bring comfort? They are the symbols of a well-prepared shepherd and provide him with a clear identity. The rod speaks of protection; and the staff is for the prodding necessary to keep the flock together and on the path.

One or more of these implements was often used to symbolize authority among ancient Near Eastern kings. Compare, for example, the use of the crook and flail in Egypt as symbols of royal authority.

In the light of the Lord's sovereign power, the mere presence of the rod and staff was enough to bring comfort to David. They symbolized the greatness of his Shepherd and confirmed His identity. The rod and staff represented protection and guidance. He was assured of rescue, if it were necessary.

David knew well the drama involved in the rescue of a wounded or lost sheep. The rod would serve to ward off any animals which might attack while the shepherd was moving toward the helpless animal. The staff provided the steadying force for the shepherd as he would often climb the sides of dangerous mountains. Anees T. Baroody provides a moving description of such a rescue.

> Here I beg to call your attention to one sheep in that busily-moving flock. It is a strong sheep and is accustomed to venture to little secluded corners and very steep places where often the best grass is found. There it is grazing by itself. One tuft after another disappears before its sharp teeth. After an hour or two this bold sheep looks around for its comrades and finds them not. It runs in all directions bleating as hard as it can, but no shepherd's voice comes back in response. At last, while darting blindly around, it falls over a precipice. Dazed and wounded it lies among the rocks.

As the evening draws near the poor creature begins to shake from terror. The wolves are howling on the other side of the valley. It cannot be more than a few hours before they find it out. It can see the wild glare of the eyes of those rapacious beasts; it can see their terrible drawn-out tongues; it can see their bloody teeth which have been sharpened by gnawing the bones of other animals. In such a miserable condition of fright, the poor sheep lies awaiting its inevitable doom.

. . . what does the shepherd do? Toward eventide he counts the sheep and, to his great astonishment, he finds only ninety and nine. He counts them over and over again. One is missing, one is missing! After taking two or three sweeping glances at the flock, he ascertains which is the missing one. . . . Our tenderhearted shepherd cannot bear to gaze long at such an agonizing picture of loss. There he leaves the ninety and nine in a safe place in the wilderness and goes back to search for the lost sheep. Watch him as he reaches the first valley. There he fells a wolf with one blow of his heavy-headed rod. . . . He runs from one rock to another looking into every ditch and every corner and every crag and every cave, until at last he reaches a low rugged precipice and, peeping down, he sees the poor creature lying between two rocks. In its desperate struggle it has wounded itself in several places. On seeing the shepherd it trembles and bleats faintly. But he does not strike it for straying, he does not reproach it, he does not utter a single unkindly word, he does not even frown at it. Stooping down, he takes hold of it by its legs, lifts it up, lays it gently on his shoulders, and starts home rejoicing. The blood trickles from its wounds upon his shoulders, but that does not annoy him. He loves the sheep, and now his joy over the finding of it is unbounded.[9]

What a graphic picture of the plight of weak and helpless sheep. Yes, there is danger in the journey, but the presence of the Shepherd guarantees the safety of the sheep even though they might recklessly wander off.

But none of the righteous ever knew
How deep were the waters crossed,
Or how dark was the night that the Lord passed through,

A shepherd gently brings back the lost, injured sheep. Matson Photo Service.

Ere he found the sheep that was lost.
Out in the desert he heard his cry,
Sick and helpless and ready to die.

Lord, whence are those blood drops all the way
That mark out the mountain track?
They were shed for the one who had gone astray,
Ere the shepherd could bring him back.
Lord, whence are thy hands so rent and torn?
They were pierced tonight by many a thorn.

(Elizabeth D. Clephane)

8

---

cA Gracious Host

The excitement in the dark eyes of Mohammad Yaseen's two boys, along with the frenzied activity around the large, black tent, were clear evidence that this night would be special. Mohammad and I had spent an enlightening and profitable week in the rugged hills of Judah with his flock of sheep and goats. The experiences of our journey included moments of great anxiety as well as periods of the greatest serenity and rest. Even though our travels were profitable, it was very evident that Mohammad was glad to be back home.

In my travels in various parts of the world, I have encountered all types of hospitality, but none that quite equaled the warmth and completeness of that offered by bedouin Arabs who roam the wilderness near Tekoa.

The encampment around Mohammad's tent included seven other tents—all belonging to various brothers or other near relatives. Each family was involved in special preparations for the evening feast. Time and time again, Mohammad reminded me that I was now a "brother" in the family and should receive the appropriate honor. I wandered around the tents watching both men and women at work and was intrigued by the great efficiency involved in the preparation of food. Nothing was wasted, and the greatest utilization was made of even the most insignificant of objects.

One of Mohammad's brothers invited me to go with him to witness the slaughter of a goat which would be prepared for the evening meal. I accepted the invitation with interest, since I had on many occasions skinned and prepared the meat of wild deer. In fact, as we approached the rocky area where the goat was to be slaughtered, I asked if I could have the privilege of skinning the animal to show them how the process is done in America. The look on the faces of the four men gathered there was that of total amazement. After all, Americans, to many of these people, consist of overweight men with short pants, gaudy shirts and a selection of cameras around their necks. The very idea of an American skinning a goat and preparing it for a meal was a stunning revelation.

The men called their friends and before the process even began there were more than 30 gathered around to watch this unusual sight. I had no idea that I was involving myself in a desert theatrical performance, but that's the way it turned out! I went about my task with what I considered efficiency and dispatch. Finally, the animal was properly skinned and pieces cut, much to the delight of my audience. A number of the men complimented me on my skill and carefulness, which was an encouragement because on hunting trips with my American colleagues, I did not always receive such praise.

Only casually did I note the fact that every part of the animal was kept by the ladies. Later that evening, I discovered that very little of a goat is discarded for any reason. As the sun began to set, the men of the encampment gathered to Mohammad's tent and we all sat around a large circle on a beautiful oriental rug with surrounding pillows.

The Bedouin shepherd's tent. Photo by Harold Mare

Conversation centered on the experiences of the past week along with the plans of the family to move their settlement to a more suitable grazing area. In a short time, the ladies had finished preparations of the food. A large platter of rice, eggplant and pieces of goat meat were placed in the middle of our group and it looked delicious. I noticed that none began to reach for the food; they appeared to be waiting for additional service.

Eventually, a young man did make his appearance with a separate platter. It had a modest amount of rice and chopped eggplant, but on the top was the head of a goat—clearly less attractive than it had appeared earlier in the day. This part of the animal, along with other portions, was considered a delicacy and was reserved for the special guest—namely, me. Let it be noted that I am a genuine fan of wild and domestic meats of all kinds. In hunting, fishing and trapping in the woods, my stomach has been treated to a wide variety of good and bad dishes. But I will have to admit that the sight of this boiled goat's head on the pile of rice was a clear culinary challenge to my stomach! Also distressing was the fact that we were more than 50 miles away from the nearest supply of Alka Seltzer!

As is often the case, the *appearance* of the food was far worse than the actual *taste*. The whole dinner proved to be a delight and I got along famously, with both food and my friends. I have described all of this to point out that there were two sides to my shepherd friend, Mohammad Yaseen. I had witnessed his rugged individualism in the wilderness of Judah as he cared for the sheep and goats. Now I was able to watch him in the role of a gracious host and provider. It was still the same man, the same shepherd, but with new circumstances.

This leads us to a consideration of Psalm 23:5, which literally reads, "You prepare a table before me in the presence of my adversaries: you anoint my head with oil; my cup is well filled."[1] As noted in an earlier discussion,[2] there is divided opinion as to the number of metaphors employed by David in the psalm.

Some scholars have argued that only one metaphor is used throughout the psalm, and that relates to the shepherd and his sheep. To interpret the psalm with more than one metaphor destroys the impact of the poem, in their view.

> Unquestionably, Ps. 23 would be stronger and more direct and effective, and its unity more profound, were the figure of the Deity, as the Good Shepherd, manifest beyond all question in vv. 1-4, maintained throughout the entire psalm. And even more disturbing and inexplicable, . . . is the reference to the enemies, in v. 5, to confound whom the generous host spreads in their presence the sumptuous banquet for his guest.[3]

This single-metaphor view is defended by E. Power,[4] W. A. Knight,[5] Robert T. Ketcham,[6] Phillip Keller[7] and Stuart Briscoe.[8]

This viewpoint, though popular, does present some difficulties. When the shepherd-sheep metaphor is applied to verses 5 and 6, absurdities develop. Stuart Briscoe struggled to turn such difficulties into some sort of spiritual benefit.

I get the wildest picture in my mind when I read v. 5 of this psalm. The old sheep is seated at a sumptuous sheep feast. The table is laden with all that a sheep could ever wish to eat. All around are wolves, licking their chops, growling and yapping. The sheep, however, is quite unperturbed. "Don't bother me, can't you see I'm busy."[9]

Others have seen this difficulty, but have chosen not to paint such a superficial picture. Clearly, the presence of a "table" is a difficulty for those maintaining a single-figure view. Keller attempts to unify the passage by citing the fact that in the western United States and southern Europe the high plateaus of sheep-ranges are referred to as *mesas,* the Spanish word for "tables." He further notes that a similar word is employed in Africa for the word "table." His conclusion on the matter is as follows:

So it may be seen that what David referred to as a table was actually the entire high summer range. Though these "mesas" may have been remote and hard to reach, the energetic and aggressive sheep owner takes the time and trouble to ready them for the arrival of his flocks.[10]

This attempt to harmonize the word "table" with the shepherd-sheep motif of the first four verses is creative enough, but it falls far short of a sober interpretation of the Biblical material. It especially should be noted that during the summer months in Palestine the highlands are hardly the place for long-term grazing. Shepherd and sheep are usually found in those valley areas that have some water resources which support the growth of vegetation. The hills of Palestine are usually quite barren and devoid of significant amounts of vegetation during the hot summer months.

The most popular interpretation of verses 5 and following is that a new image is introduced—namely, that of a host and his guest. More specifically, a number of writers associate this scene with a wealthy host and his provisions for an oriental banquet. Leupold observes: "The limits of the figure are not strictly maintained, for it might seem to come closer to the figure of an oriental banquet when the second member of the verse speaks of the anointing with (perfumed) oil, a courtesy shown guests at a banquet in early times."[11] E. Vogt agrees to a change in metaphor, but feels that:

> The poet does not represent God under the figure of a bountiful host; nay, God is really the Psalmist's host in the temple, because the sacrificial meal is offered as a gift by God to him who in turn had offered God the victim and his own devotion . . . we are dealing here with the thanksgiving banquet and that this implies that the Psalmist has passed quite recently through a grave danger and trouble.[12]

While a large majority of commentators agree to a second figure in the psalm, there is considerable difference of opinion as to whether it is the general figure of a host and guest, a king in a royal banquet setting, or a thanksgiving feast.

If the transition in verse 5 is to a royal palace or the sacred temple, it would be an abrupt change indeed, especially in the light of the brevity of our psalm. It would appear to this writer that the change is not one of figure, but setting. In the case of verse 5, we do not see the shepherd in the fields with his flocks, but back at his tents with a guest. Such a picture is not out of harmony with oriental practice or custom. Many Palestinian shepherds are comparatively wealthy and are capable of providing a dinner of exquisite quality. This was effectively illustrated by my experience in the tents of Mohammad Yaseen. With this approach, we are not faced with such a radical change in the imagery of the passage and yet the distinctive elements of verse 5 can be interpreted literally without resorting to allegorical approaches or textual emendation.

In the previous chapter, we noted that the emphasis of verses 4 and 5 in this psalm related to the protection provided by the shepherd. The *nature* and *extent* of the Lord's protection was observed to be the emphasis of verse 4, whereas verse 5 focused on the *benefits* of His protection. This concept is developed by David in three lines of thought.

I. The Circumstances of Blessing

The impact of this delightful little psalm increases in both breadth and depth with the sentiments of verse 5. Earlier, David viewed believers as sheep in desperate need of the Lord's protection, guidance and provision. But the blessings of the Lord had so overwhelmed David that he chose a new setting to describe them. Looking at the perfect Shepherd now as a host, he declared, "You prepare a table before me in the presence of my adversaries."[13]

Even though David creates a new setting for the truth he is about to present, the principal ideas of the passage are continued—for the traveler was just as much in need of guidance, protection and provision as were the sheep.

In our modern age of paved highways, rapid travel, good lights and sophisticated communication, it might seem strange for us to conceive of a traveler being so vulnerable or helpless. But in ancient Palestine where he was required to travel rugged roads and narrow paths through forested regions, he could easily have been robbed and beaten. The journey from Jerusalem to Jericho was filled with dangers because thieves and robbers were easily concealed in the rugged, barren hills of that region. Jesus alluded to this kind of situation in the parable of the good Samaritan: "A certain man went down from Jerusalem to Jericho, and fell among thieves, which stripped him of his raiment, and wounded him, and departed, leaving him half dead" (Luke 10:30). That kind of incident was not isolated. It was well known that the hills of that region were favorite lurking places for thieves.

There are two recorded incidents in the Old Testament that illustrate well the obligations and concerns of a good host. Upon meeting two travelers, Lot encouraged them to come to his house and remain for the night. When they entered his house "he made them a feast, and did bake unleavened bread, and they did eat" (Gen. 19:3). That night, however, wicked men from the city of Sodom came to his house demanding that the guests be given to these men to gratify their perverted desires. Lot, recognizing his obligation as a host to protect these men at any cost, offered his daughters rather than allow his guests to be abused (19:8). To a modern Westerner, such a decision seems incredible, but to an Oriental who appreciates the obligation of a host to protect his guest, there is a measure of understanding and sympathy.

A very similar occurrence is recorded in the nineteenth chapter of Judges. A Levite was traveling and found friendly lodging in the house of an Ephraimite (Judges 19:15-21). As they were enjoying the meal, certain "sons of Belial" came to his house demanding that the Levite be given to them for sexual gratification (19:22). The expression "sons of Belial" refers to worthless, base men of the community. In this case, the host refused to permit the abuse of his guest and gave his daughter to them (19:24). These two accounts give us some indication of the tremendous responsibility assumed by a host for his guest.

Abraham, a tent-dwelling, semi-nomad, also offered warm hospitality for travelers he met. The details of Genesis 18 provide an excellent background for our understanding of the shepherd as a host. It will be remembered that Abraham was noted for the large flocks and herds which he possessed.

Of course, not everyone who entertained in the Old Testament was the epitome of kindness and gentleness. We remember very vividly the rather unique reception given to the Canaanite general Sisera when he fled during the battle against the armies of Israel. On his way away from the battleground, he was invited by Jael, the wife of a Kenite, to come to the tent for a rest and refreshment (Judges 4:17-18). After his appetite was cared for, he lay down to sleep, and while asleep Jael took a tent peg and nailed his skull to the ground (Judges 4:21). The Biblical text rather anti-climactically adds, "So he died." It is very evident that the alliance that Jael's husband, Heber, had developed between himself and the Canaanites was not acceptable to her.

We now return to the Twenty-Third Psalm and the important features of verse 5.

A. The Prepared Table. The use of the expression
"table" in this verse has created considerable difficulty for
those interpreters who attempt to maintain a strict shepherd-
sheep setting for the whole chapter. In what possible manner
would sheep be eating from a table in a pastoral context?
Keller suggests that the Biblical "table" was really a word that
alluded to "the entire high summer range." But this
explanation was based on a Spanish word which has no
relationship either to the Hebrew text or oriental pastoral
practices in Palestine.

A popular approach to the difficulty is to relate the Hebrew
word *šulḥān* ("table") to the Arabic word *salaḥa* ("to strip off
the hide").[15] The object depicted, then, would be a "skin or
leather mat spread on the ground"[16] on which the shepherd
would place food for the sheep. I spoke with both
Mohammad Yaseen and Abas Tawfeek about this practice
and they were not aware that shepherds commonly did this.
Mohammad did mention the fact that occasionally he would
place a cloth on the ground and place food on it for small
lambs which might be too timid to feed with the others. Abas
related one occasion when he took a bag of feed along with
his other possessions on the back of a donkey in order to
provide feed for a couple of animals which were not eating
well. W. A. Knight depicts such a scene in his little booklet,
The Song of Our Syrian Guest.[17] But in the light of our
context and the words that follow, it seems unlikely that the
activities described would naturally apply to sheep. Mention
of both table and cup speak of a dinner scene involving
people, rather than animals.

Furthermore, recent evidence would seem to point to the
fact that the Hebrew word *šulḥān* should not be traced to an
Arabic root, but to the Ugaritic word *ṯlḥn* which means
"table."[18] This new evidence, however, does not demand that
a large sophisticated wooden table is in view, for such an
object would be quite out of place in the tent of even the
wealthiest of shepherds. Wooden furniture and other large
objects are not characteristic of either nomadic or semi-

nomadic tent-dwellers. Items found in these seating areas normally include rugs and pillows, but not large tables or chairs.

In the context of a shepherd caring for his guest at the tent, therefore, what did David mean that the Lord "prepares a table"? The expression he used was a common formula for the furnishing of a meal without specific reference to any furniture involved. For example, Proverbs 9:2 has this to say about the wife: "She hath killed her beasts; she hath mingled her wine; *she hath also furnished her table.*"[19] Whether she had a literal table, a special mat spread on the floor of the tent, or a pillow to hold the metal platter is beside the point. The idea conveyed by the expression "furnished her table" is that she faithfully provided meals for her family.

The Lord, as the Perfect Shepherd, not only knows the needs and hungers of wandering sheep, but He also anticipates the desires of His guest. David was not dealing in mere repetition of thought by presenting a table after discussing pastures. He found himself overwhelmed by the extent of God's blessing, the nature of which went far beyond that which would be enjoyed by the sheep. Not being able to express the fullness of God's provision with a shepherd-sheep image, he turned our attention to the large tent of the shepherd and his graciousness as a host. It is only against this Near Eastern background that we can fully appreciate the scope of his emphasis.

Roland de Vaux described the role of the desert host in this manner:

> Hospitality . . . is a necessity of life in the desert, but among the nomads this necessity has become a virtue, and a most highly esteemed one. The guest is sacred: the honor of providing for him is disputed, but generally falls to the sheikh. The stranger can avail himself of his hospitality for three days, and after leaving he has a right to protection for a given time.[20]

It is characteristic of bedouin Arabs to select the very best food they have available for the guest. How well I remember the frenzied activity around the tents of Abas Tawfeek as they sought to provide the best meal possible for me. While the food of the tent-dwelling nomad is limited, we are reminded that the Perfect Shepherd suffers no limitations whatsoever. All that we might require is fully supplied by the One who has redeemed us.

One other view of this phrase in verse 5 is worthy of examination. E. Power felt that the image of the shepherd should be maintained throughout the entire passage. He, like others, has struggled with the reference to a table. In order to maintain the sheep-shepherd image throughout the chapter, he has chosen to emend the Hebrew text so that the word *šulḥān* is read *šlḥ* which means "weapons." He would then render the phrase, "thou preparest (or bearest) before me weapons against my enemies." It is his view that the Masoretic text has suffered from dittography. It is suggested that the final *nun* on the Hebrew word *šulḥān* . . . "owes its origin to a dittography of the initial letter of the following word *ngd*."[21] This explanation of the verse was later followed by Julian Morgenstern,[22] but has not been widely accepted by other scholars.

While such emendation of the original text is clever enough, it seems to be quite unnecessary. The figure of a shepherd in the general sense can be maintained throughout the psalm if we recognize that there is a shift from the sheep to the guest, maintaining the theme of the Shepherd's provision.

B. The Presence of Enemies. If one maintains that shepherd and sheep are in view throughout this passage, then "the enemies are, of course, the beast of prey, such as wolves and jackals, which, particularly at night, lurk about the sheepfold seeking to snatch a sheep from the flock."[23] But if the imagery is not that of shepherd and sheep, but of the shepherd as a host with his guest, who then are the enemies? Franz Delitzsch suggests that David wrote this psalm with the memory of Absalom's rebellion in view. He points to II Samuel 17 where three men, who were not even Israelites, cared for David when he had to flee from his son Absalom. David was so impressed with the hospitality of those who protected him that he utilized that experience to illustrate God's provision even in the darkest of circumstances.

While such an association is of course possible, it is doubtful that David had any specific event in mind when penning the words of this psalm. Much of David's life was characterized by flight, fear and reliance upon the hospitality of others. Many times, both as a young lad and as a king, he

Small wild fox caught near Petra in Jordan. Levant Photo Service.

found himself dining with his enemies 'round about.

On one occasion, I spent several days in the Jordanian desert to the east, studying the responsibilities of the *Badia,* Jordan's desert patrol, for a newspaper feature.[25] After my work was complete, I decided to spend an extra day at a small oasis where a group of bedouin had gathered, along with their sheep and goats. Earlier I was warned by the desert patrol that there had been a gun battle at the site between the bedouin and a group of bandits which was roaming that region.

As I approached the encampment, I met an elderly gentleman who welcomed me to his tent and offered hot tea, which I accepted with pleasure. While we talked, other younger members of his family gathered about and related some of the harrowing experiences of the previous days. One young man told of gunmen who attempted to rob the small group of bedouin who were on their way to the market with many handmade goods, as well as sheep and goats. The robbers failed, and a number of them were wounded in the gun battle that had taken place. After spending an hour or two in conversation, I was about to leave; but immediately the host implored me to stay on for the evening meal. This I did, and it proved to be a profitable decision.

As the food was brought to the center of the tent and we were just about to begin eating, I heard shots fired from a distance. My first inclination was to look immediately for the softest soil possible to start digging a foxhole, but my host seemed unperturbed by the noise outside. Calmly, he handed me my food and said to me, "You need not worry; they are what remain of the thieves. They are angry and humiliated, but defeated. They will not harm us."

My mind has gone back to that scene on numerous occasions as I have reflected upon David's words in this verse. I am reminded that the Lord Jesus has defeated the enemy of our souls, and we are able to gather at His table with perfect freedom and peace. What a marvelous truth in an age so characterized by insecurity and uncertainty!

The discovery of the Tell el-Amarna Tablets in Egypt late in 1887 sheds interesting light on David's statement in this verse. A minor king praised the Egyptian pharaoh by saying, "May the king give gifts unto his servants while our enemies look on."[26] It would appear from this statement that for a monarch to be able to provide for his servants with enemies looking on was an evidence of his power and certainly enhanced his honor.

Our Shepherd, who is King, does provide for His own, no matter how dark the circumstances. We should also be reminded that it was in the swirling currents of Roman tyranny and Jewish hatred that Jesus gathered His own for communion and fellowship. There are many even today who gather around the Lord's table in secrecy, surrounded by those who seek their lives. Perhaps we should approach the symbols of the communion table with even greater appreciation in the light of these truths.

The minister of the Gospel often finds himself in the loneliest of situations. Surrounded by pressure and trouble, there is often the temptation to give up and abandon the ministry. This psalm should be a means of encouragement in such circumstances, for the Lord not only *can* provide strength in the most complex of life situations, but He *desires* to do so. The Apostle Paul expressed an amazing confidence in the midst of his difficulties: "We are troubled on every side, yet not distressed; we are perplexed, but not in despair; persecuted, but not forsaken; cast down, but not destroyed" (II Cor. 4:8-9).

Two times in II Corinthians 4, the Apostle Paul encouraged the minister of the Gospel not to faint (vv. 1,16). He first challenged the man of God to continue on because of the nature and the importance of the gospel ministry (v. 1). Also he viewed the problems of life, not as a means to discouragement, but as an opportunity for the renewing of the inward man day by day (v. 16).

Our engagement in spiritual battles is often so furious and lengthy that we fail to realize necessity for withdrawal for contemplation and feeding. The Lord desires to prepare a table for us even in the midst of the most distressing circumstances of life. Our responsibility is to avail ourselves of this opportunity, for it is by this means that the Lord's rich provisions are enjoyed.

II. The Certainty of Blessing

It is not enough for one merely to promise blessing and provision when enemies are 'round about. There is the matter of actual performance. David reminds us that our blessings are made certain because it is the Lord who provides for His own. It is very important that the child of God recognizes the sovereignty of his Lord. There is a great danger in current pop theology which reduces God to a backslapping big brother. Some have maintained that it is this kind of God who provides warmth and assurance. I rather doubt that. I believe that a firm emphasis on God's sovereign power and His greatness is far more practical in terms of producing assurance.

Needless to say, we must not overemphasize His sovereignty and forget the intimate, personal relationship we have with Him. The psalmist, under the inspiration of the Holy Spirit, does a remarkable job of balancing these two great truths with utmost delicacy. On one hand, he presents the transcendent Creator, the God of the heavens; and on the other hand, we meet the Lord as our Shepherd in intimate pastoral scenes. When both of these aspects of the divine relationship are properly emphasized, the believer is able to worship his Lord with confidence.

Two additional ideas emerge from the consideration of the Lord's preparations for His own. In this psalm the emphasis is on His present supply for our needs, but John refers to another preparation that anticipates the future: "And if I go and *prepare* a place for you, I will come again, and receive you unto myself; that where I am, there ye may be also" (John 14:3). We are not only moved to praise for the present provisions at the hands of a gracious host, but rejoice in anticipation for what the future holds.

III. The Completeness of Blessing

David not only described the basic provision of the gracious host with a well-prepared meal; but with two additional statements emphasizes the thoroughness of the host concerned.

A. The Anointed Head. If one takes verse 5 to be a continuation of the shepherd-sheep activity, then the anointing of the head with oil would allude to the shepherd pouring oil on the wounds of injured sheep. On the other hand, if a banquet scene is in view, the reference would be to unguents and perfumes which were common provisions of a gracious oriental host (Amos 6:6; Ps. 45:7; Ps. 92:10; Ps. 133:1-2 and Luke 7:36-50).

Anointing the head with oil is often referred to in Scripture as a sign of joy and happiness. For example, Ecclesiastes 9:8 declares, "let not oil depart from thine head," which is an encouragement to rejoice always. E. Power further points out that, "the head was regularly anointed in connection with the daily recurring ablution, except in times of fasting and sadness, and though it was customary to anoint guests there is no necessary connection between anointing and hospitality."[27]

It is true that there was no legal obligation for one to anoint the guest with perfumed oils in the oriental world, but the fact that one would do it was a sign of the sincerest form of hospitality. I cannot help but rejoice when I meditate upon this fact in the light of Psalm 23:5. The Lord not only makes full provision at His table for all of our needs, but He anoints our head with oil; that is, He provides something far beyond the requirements of a gracious host. This is grace. The Christian life is filled with blessings, all of which come as the result of His grace—and not our merit. Just be sure that we fully understand the magnitude of God's provision, David introduces a third feature of the shepherd-guest relationship, namely, the well-filled cup.

B. The Filled Cup. The identification of the "cup" here depends solely on whether or not Psalm 23 contains one or two metaphors. For those who maintain a single image throughout the psalm, "the 'cup' here is the trough or short trench, which the faithful shepherd digs in the earth or sand in close proximity to the well, in order that the sheep might drink with comfort."[28] A popular identification of this cup is the stone-cut trough that is often found next to cisterns in Palestine. The image created, then, would be of a shepherd filling the trough with water to the point of overflowing.

If, on the other hand, the imagery of David is that of a dinner provided by a loving host, the cup would be understood as the cup employed for the drinking of liquids at a dinner or banquet. Of course David is not merely referring to the provisions of food and drink in this life. His allusion is to the great spiritual benefits that we have from the Lord—and these without limit. This is the thought of Psalm 16:5, "The Lord is my choice portion and my cup," which captures nicely the original sense.[29] The metaphorical use of the word cup " . . . signifies that he is the satisfying draught that refreshes and invigorates the soul, a thought developed quite forcefully by Jesus in John 4."[30]

The cup is also commonly used in Scripture to refer to the experiences of life. Sometimes these experiences are quite bitter. Psalm 11:6 states; "Upon the wicked he shall rain snares, fire and brimstone, and an horrible tempest: this shall be the portion of their cup" (Ps. 75:8). On the other hand, this same expression is used to designate the Lord's blessing and favor. "I will take the cup of salvation and call upon the name of the Lord" (Ps. 116:13; cf. also Ps. 16:5).

The psalmist puts emphasis on the fact that the cup which we have is completely filled by the Lord. The noun *rewāyâ* is derived from the verbal root (*rāwâ*) meaning "to be saturated, or drink one's fill." Delitzsch suggests that this is a fullness which is "satiating even to excess."[31] David, in the simplest of imagery, was illustrating the fact that the Lord's provisions are full and complete. The cup of the believer will not go empty or even be inadequately filled. This magnificent thought is in perfect agreement with the Apostle Paul's declaration, "But my God shall supply all your need according to his riches in glory by Christ Jesus" (Phil. 4:19).

The spirit of Psalm 23:5 was more than adequately captured by the little girl who went home after Sunday School and reported on her studies of the morning: "I don't remember what all the lesson was about, but we did study the verse in the Old Testament that said, 'Mercy Goodness my cup's runned over.'"

There is clearly something wrong with the individual who can read this fifth verse of the Twenty-Third Psalm and not be prompted to praise his God. The scene begins with the careful preparation of the host for the needs of his guest. The power of the host and his defeat of all surrounding enemies make the scene one of peace and comfort. He goes far beyond the minimal requirements of graciousness, with the provisions of perfumes and oils—and it does not end there. The cup is filled to the brim with the promise of more if it is needed. What David does not adequately portray with a pastoral scene on the hillsides, he does with the shepherd as a host in the tent.

The shepherd with his flute in the wilderness of Judah. Matson Photo Service.

9

The Believer's Prospect

Psalm 23:6

It should come as no surprise that the sixth string on David's harp should sound a note of confidence and assurance. He has taken us through deep ravines, dark valleys, barren hillsides—and in all situations the Shepherd has faithfully cared for His own. No wild animal or thief has been able to destroy the life of either sheep or lamb.

As we move to the concluding note of David's magnificent melody, it strikes our ears with rich, spiritual tones. As helpless sheep, we have followed Him and have found the way sure. When it appeared that a barren world would deprive us of life-sustaining food, He fed us. When our bones ached with weariness from difficult journeys, He faithfully provided resting places, rich with pasture and a good supply of water.

We also followed our perfect Shepherd, not as sheep, but as guests to His tent, only to realize even greater blessing and full provision. In spite of surrounding turmoil, we ate in peace at a table with an endless supply of blessings. Anointed and with a full cup, we rejoiced in the goodness of our divine host. David's simple shepherd-song now builds into a symphonic crescendo of theological richness. What he says in this concluding verse of Psalm 23 is not unexpected. With startling brevity, he is able to capture the totality of divine blessing and give us a clue to his own heart's desire.

I. The Promise of Temporal Blessing

In order to capture our attention, David began this final verse with an interesting particle to emphasize the truth at hand. The Hebrew word $^{\circ}ak$ is in an emphatic positon and may be translated either "only" or "surely." Alexander prefers the former rendering, with this explanation: "The favor which he shall experience is so great that he regards it as unmixed, or the exceptions as unworthy of consideration."[1]

While the above translation is certainly grammatically possible, it is doubtful that it should be preferred. Surely David knew that the remaining days of his life would be characterized by some difficulty and disappointment. He was emphasizing the assurance of God's continued blessing and care in spite of all circumstances.

What exactly was it of which he was assured? The Hebrew word $\underline{t}\hat{o}\underline{b}$ ("goodness") is a common expression referring to good fortune or welfare. David knew well that whatever good he had in life was from the Lord: "I say to the Lord, 'thou art my Lord; I have no good apart from thee'" (Ps. 16:2 RSV). The same sentiment is expressed in Psalm 73:25, "Whom have I in heaven but thee? and there is none upon earth that I desire besides thee."

David not only expected goodness from the Lord, but steadfast love as well. The Hebrew word *ḥesed* is one of the richest words in the Old Testament. It has been variously translated "covenant loyalty," "loving kindness" and "steadfast love." It is a term that has deep covenant associations with it. Of its 278 appearances in the Old Testament, more than 150 have some clear association with a covenant idea.[2] David, therefore, was assured in his mind that blessing and steadfast love would be his because of the greatness of his Shepherd.

The verb chosen by David to describe this experience is most interesting. It is the Hebrew verb *rādap*, meaning "to pursue or chase someone." It is often used in Scripture in a battle context, with troops pursuing each other. David was simply emphasizing the fact that blessing will follow good men just as surely as judgment will follow evil men.

Unlike those of governments, politicians and even educators, these promises will be enduring. The expression "all the days of my life" is better translated "days without end."[3] This clearly refers to lifelong blessing and supply from God; but that was not the total extent of David's prospects for the future.

III. The Assurance of Eternal Blessing

David's great desire was not only to be the beneficiary of divine favor, but to be able to dwell in the presence of his Lord forever. The verbal form translated "and I will dwell" is problematical. As it is currently pointed in the Hebrew text, the translation should be "and I will return to the house of the Lord" for its root would be *šûb*. Others have chosen to take the word in the Hebrew text as a defective writing for the root *yāšab* meaning "to sit or dwell."[4] More recently, Mitchell Dahood has demonstrated that the Masoretic text can be maintained without surrendering the idea of sitting or dwelling.[5] The idea of dwelling in the house of the Lord or in His presence seems most appropriate for the text at hand.

The very mention of the "house of the Lord" has led many to conclude that this is a reference to the temple—and therefore could not have been written by David. But surely such an interpretation is arbitrary. In the specific sense, David might well have been alluding to the presence of the Lord as symbolized by the Ark of the Covenant and the

Hospitality in an Arab Bedouin tent. Andrews University Archaeological Expedition to Tell Hisban, Paul H. Denton, photographer.

temporary dwelling that surrounded it. This, in his day, was an important place of worship, especially when he removed the Ark of Jerusalem to give it central importance. But David's concept of God's presence certainly went beyond the localized area of a building, a temple or a tabernacle. He was perfectly capable of envisioning the presence of God wherever communion was possible.

There is little doubt that the tabernacle, and later the temple, had special significance to the Israelite with respect to God's presence. To pray at or worship in the temple was something greatly desired.

"Lord, I have loved the habitation of thy house, and the place where thine honour dwelleth" (Ps. 26:8).

"One thing have I desired of the Lord, that will I seek after; that I may dwell in the house of the Lord all the days of my life, to behold the beauty of the Lord, and to inquire of his temple" (Ps. 27:4).

"Blessed is the man whom thou choosest, and causest to approach unto thee, that he may dwell in thy courts: we shall be satisfied with the goodness of thy house, even thy holy temple" (Ps. 65:4).[6]

The longing of the Christian's heart is not merely to worship in a church, or to sing in a cathedral, but to enjoy the actual presence of the Lord forever. The Lord Jesus promised that He was preparing a place for us, that where He was we might be also (John 14:3). The deep longing of the believer's heart is to be in the presence of his redeemer forever.

Like David, we do not merely state this truth as a vague wish, but as a certain prospect. Literally translated, David said, "And my dwelling will be in the house of the Lord forever." It is with that same assurance that the child of God looks forward to the prospect of heaven.

It is not accidental that our psalm begins with the Lord's name and concludes with it as well. The emphasis of the song is upon the perfect Shepherd—namely, the Lord. Whatever the sheep has and whatever the guest enjoys is the result of God's grace. In verses 1 through 3, we saw *our provisions;* while verses 4 and 5 emphasized *our protection.* The final verse was a highlight of *our prospect*—both in this life and in the life to come.

As we view the character of the perfect Shepherd, we must conclude that since He leads, the way is sure, since He cares, the way is safe; and since He feeds, the way is sweet.

Notes

CHAPTER 1

[1]Charles H. Spurgeon, *Psalms* (Grand Rapids: Kregel Publications, 1968), p. 107.

[2]A. Maclaren, *The Psalms,* Vol. I *The Expositor's Bible,* ed. W. Robertson Nicoll (New York: Funk and Wagnalls Company, 1900), p. 226.

[3]See D. Barthelemy and J. T. Milik, *Qumran Cave I. Discoveries in the Judaean Desert, I* (Oxford: 1955), p. 133.

[4]H. C. Leupold, *Exposition of the Psalms* (Minneapolis: Augsburg Publishing House, 1959), p. 1.

[5]For examples of this name change, compare Ps. 14:2 with Ps. 53:2; and Ps. 40:13-17 with Ps. 70:1-5.

[6]A. S. Rappoport, *The Psalms in Life, Legend and Literature* (London: The Centenary Press, 1935), p. 37.

CHAPTER 2

[1]On the various uses of *lāmeḏ,* see Mitchell Dahood, *Ugaritic-Hebrew Philology* (Rome: Pontifical Biblical Institute, 1965), p. 25.

[2]See Gleason L. Archer, *A Survey of Old Testament Introduction* (Chicago: Moody Press, 1964), p. 435 and E. J. Young, *Introduction to the Old Testament* (Grand Rapids: Wm. B. Eerdmans Publishing Company, 1949), p. 297. Also compare Ludwig Koehler and Walter Baumgartner, *Lexicon in Veteris Testamenti Libros* (Leiden: E. J. Brill, 1958), pp. 259-60.

[3]For further discussion of David's authorship, see J. G. S. S. Thompson, "Psalms, Book of," *The New Bible Dictionary*, ed. J. D. Douglas (Grand Rapids: Wm. B. Eerdmans Publishing Company, 1962), p. 1053.

[4]William R. Taylor and W. Stewart McCullough, *The Psalms: The Interpreter's Bible*, Vol. IV ed. George A. Buttrick (New York: Abingdon Press, 1955), p. 124.

[5]W. O. E. Oesterley, *The Psalms* (London: S. P. C. K., 1962), p. 183.

[6]Charles A. and Emilie G. Briggs, *The Book of Psalms*, Vol. I (New York: Charles Scribner's Sons, 1914), p. 208.

[7]Franz Delitzsch, *Biblical Commentary on the Psalms*, Vol. I (Grand Rapids: Wm. B. Eerdmans Publishing Company, n.d.) p. 329 and J. J. Stewart Perowne, *The Book of Psalms*, Vol. I (Grand Rapids: Zondervan Publishing House, 1966), p. 249.

[8]Phillip Keller, *A Shepherd Looks at Psalm 23* (Grand Rapids: Zondervan Publishing House, 1970), pp. 104ff. Also see Julian Morgenstern, "Psalm 23," *Journal of Biblical Literature*, 65:1 (March 1946), 13-24.

[9]*Ibid.*, p. 104.

[10]J. J. Stewart Perowne, *op. cit.*, p. 249.

[11]W. Graham Scroggie, *The Psalms* (Old Tappan, New Jersey: Fleming H. Revell Company, 1965), p. 145.

[12]J. Sidlow Baxter, *Explore the Book*, Vol. III (Grand Rapids: Zondervan Publishing House, 1960), pp. 126-127.

[13]P. Volz, "Psalm 23," *Neue Kirchliche Zeitschrift*, 36 (1925), 576ff.

CHAPTER 3

[1]J. N. Postgate, "Some Old Babylonian Shepherds and Their Flocks," *Journal of Semitic Studies*, 20:1 (Spring 1975), 6.

[2]*Ibid.*

[3]"The Code of Hammurabi," *Ancient Near Eastern Texts*, trans. Theophile J. Meek, ed. James B. Pritchard (Princeton: Princeton University Press, 1955), p. 177, paragraph 267. (Hereafter referred to as *ANET.*)

[4]Also compare Isaiah 56:11; Zechariah 11:5, 16; Ezekiel 22:25.

[5]Other references to the dangers posed by wild animals are found in Isaiah 31:4; Jeremiah 5:6 and Amos 3:12.

[6]Eric F. F. Bishop, "The Door of the Sheep," *The Expository Times*, 71:10 (July-October 1960), 307.

[7]Joachim Boessneck and Angela von den Driesch, "Preliminary Analysis of the Animal Bones from Ḥesbân," *Andrews University Seminary Studies,* 26:1 (Spring 1978), 270.

[8]W. M. Thomson, *The Land and the Book* (London: T. Nelson and Sons, 1903), p. 203.

[9]"The Code of Hammurabi," *ANET, op. cit.,* p. 164.

[10]C. J. Mullo Weir, "Letters from Tell-El-Amarna," *Documents from Old Testament Times,* ed. D. Winton Thomas (New York: Harper and Row, 1961), p. 43.

[11]D. D. Luckenbill, *Ancient Records of Assyria and Babylonia* (Chicago: University of Chicago Press, 1926), pp. 38, 50, 54, 56, 62, 63, 65, 73, 88, 139-40, 158, 169, 171, 173, 184, 190 and 193ff. My appreciation is expressed to Prof. Donald L. Fowler for calling these references to my attention.

[12]R. T. Rundle Clark, *Myth and Symbol in Ancient Egypt,* (London: Thomas and Hudson, 1959), pp. 68-70.

[13]See J. J. Glück, "Nagid-Shepherd," *Vetus Testamentum,* 13:2 (April 1963), 144.

CHAPTER 4

[1]Ray C. Stedman, *Folk Psalms of Faith* (Glendale, California: Regal Books, 1973), pp. 80-81.

[2]Stuart Briscoe, *What Works When Life Doesn't* (Wheaton: Victor Books, 1967), p. 71.

[3]*Fauna and Flora of the Bible* (London: United Bible Societies, 1972), p. 75.

[4]*Ibid.*

[5]Anees T. Baroody, *The Syrian Shepherd* (Chicago: Privately printed, 1916), p. 22.

CHAPTER 5

[1]Author's translation.

[2]See Francis Brown, S. R. Driver and Charles Briggs, *A Hebrew and English Lexicon* (Oxford: The Clarendon Press, 1952), p. 627. (Hereafter referred to as *BDB*). Also see Ludwig Koehler and Walter Baumgartner, *Lexicon in Veteris Testamenti Libros* (Leiden: E. J. Brill, 1958), p. 601.

[3]Victor P. Hamilton, "The Shepherd Psalm: Psalm 23," *The Asbury Seminarian,* 26:1 (January 1972), 6.

[4]Joseph A. Alexander, *The Psalms* (Grand Rapids: n.d.), p. 108. Also see H. C. Leupold, *Exposition of the Psalms* (Minneapolis: Augsburg Publishing House, 1959), p. 211.

[5]Ray C. Stedman, *op. cit.,* p. 82.

[6]O. E. Phillips, *Exploring the Messianic Psalms* (Philadelphia, Pennsylvania: Hebrew Christian Fellowship, Inc., 1967), pp. 79-84.

CHAPTER 6

[1]The translation of the Authorized Version "converting the soul" for the Hebrew *m^ešîbat nāpeš* in this context is unfortunate. The preferred rendering for the verb *šûb* is "restoring" or "refreshing" as in Psalm 23:3.

[2]Robert T. Ketcham, *I Shall Not Want* (Chicago: Moody Press, 1953), p. 26.

[3]Author's translation.

CHAPTER 7

[1]Author's translation.

[2]H. C. Leupold, *op. cit.*, p. 212. See also J. J. Stewart Perowne, *op. cit.*, pp. 252-53.

[3]Franz Delitzsch, *op. cit.*, p. 330-331.

[4]D. W. Thomas, "Ṣalmawet in the Old Testament," *Journal of Semitic Studies* (1962), 191-200.

[5]Mitchell Dahood, "Psalms I (1-50)," *The Anchor Bible* (Garden City, New York: Doubleday and Company, Inc., 1966), p. 147.

[6]H. C. Leupold, *op. cit.*, p. 213.

[7]Author's translation.

[8]George M. Mackie, *Bible Manners and Customs* (New York: Fleming H. Revell Company, n.d.), p. 31. For a full discussion of the rod and its uses, see E. Power, "The Shepherd's Two Rods in Modern Palestine and in Some Passages of the Old Testament," *Biblica,* 9 (1928), 434-442.

[9]Anees T. Baroody, *The Syrian Shepherd* (Chicago: Privately printed, 1916), pp. 53-59.

[10]James Stalker, *The Psalm of Psalms* (New York: Charles Scribner's Sons, 1913), p. 27.

CHAPTER 8

[1]Author's translation.

[2]See pp. 31-34.

[3]Julian Morgenstern, *op. cit.*, 15.

[4]E. Power, *op. cit.*, 439.

[5]W. A. Knight, *The Song of Our Syrian Guest* (Stirling, Scotland: Stirling Tract Enterprise, n.d.), pp. 10-14.

[6]Robert T. Ketcham, *op. cit.*, pp. 40-56.

[7]Phillip Keller, *op. cit.*, pp. 104-126.

[8]Stuart Briscoe, *op. cit.*, pp. 77.

[9]*Ibid.*

[10]Phillip Keller, *op. cit.,* p. 105.

[11]H. C. Leupold, *op. cit.,* p. 213. See also Victor P. Hamilton, *op. cit.,* 9; Franz Delitzsch, *op. cit.,* p. 331; Derek Kidner, *Psalms 1-72* (London: Tyndale Press, 1973), pp. 111-12 and A. A. Anderson, *The Book of Psalms, The New Century Bible* I (London: Marshall, Morgan and Scott, 1972), p. 198.

[12]E. Vogt, *op. cit.,* 201-2.

[13]Author's translation.

[14]Phillip Keller, *op cit.,* p. 105.

[15]See Mitchell Dahood, *Psalms I* (1-50), *The Anchor Bible* (New York: Doubleday and Company, Inc., 1955), p. 147.

[16]Francis Brown, S. R. Driver and Charles Briggs, *op. cit.,* p. 1020.

[17]W. A. Knight, *op, cit.,* photo opposite p. 9.

[18]Cyrus H. Gordon, *Ugaritic Textbook: Glossary and Indices* (Rome: Pontificium Institutum Biblicum, 1967), p. 502 (No. 2681). See also Mitchell Dahood, *op. cit.,* p. 147.

[19]Compare also Isaiah 21:5 and Ezekiel 23:41.

[20]Roland de Vaux, *Ancient Israel* (New York: McGraw-Hill Book Company, 1965) I:10.

[21]E. Power, *op. cit.,* 439.

[22]Julian Morgenstern, *op. cit.,* 15-17.

[23]*Ibid.,* 17.

[24]Franz Delitzsch, *op. cit.,* p. 331. Also see Ray Stedman, *op. cit.,* p. 90-91.

[25]For the author's account of the organization and duties of Jordan's desert patrol, see: "Jordan's Badia Patrol: Dust and Danger," *Warsaw Times-Union,* Aug. 5, 1976, p. 9.

[26]El Amarna text 100, lines 33-35. J. A. Knudtzon, *Die El-Amarna-Tafeln* I (Aalen: Otto Zeller Verlagsbuchhandlung, 1964), p. 453. Also see Mitchell Dahood, *op. cit.,* pp. 147-148.

[27]E. Power, *op. cit.,* 440, footnote 2.

[28]Julian Morgenstern, *op. cit.,* 18.

[29]H. C. Leupold, *op. cit.,* p. 149.

[30]*Ibid.*

[31]Franz Delitzsch, *op. cit.,* p. 331.

CHAPTER 9

[1]Joseph A. Alexander, *op. cit.,* p. 109. See also E. Power, *op. cit.,* 440.

[2]For recent studies on this word see Nelson Glueck, *Hesed in the Bible,* trans. Alfred Gottschalk, ed. Elias L. Epstein (New York: Ktav Publishing House, 1975) and R. B. Laurin, "The Meaning of Chesedh," *Foundations,* VII:2 (April 1964), 179-82.

[3]The Hebrew reads $le^{\supset}\bar{o}re\underline{k}$ $y\bar{a}m\hat{i}m$ "for length of days" which Mitchell Dahood understands as "eternal life," *op. cit.*, p. 149.

[4]In this case *ša$\underline{b}$tî* is merely a defective writing of *ši$\underline{b}$tî*, an infinitive form with a first-person suffix.

[5]Mitchell Dahood, *op. cit.*, p. 148.

[6]Compare also Psalms 36:7-9 and 84:2-3.

Bibliography

Books

Alexander, Joseph A. *The Psalms*. Grand Rapids: Zondervan Publishing House, n.d. Reprint of 1864 edition.

Alexander, William. *The Witness of the Psalms to Christ and Christianity*. New York: E. P. Dutton and Company, 1877.

Anderson, A. A. *The Book of Psalms*. *New Century Bible*, edited by Ronald E. Clements, Vol. I. Greenwood, South Carolina: The Attic Press, 1972.

Anderson, Bernard W. *Out of the Depths: The Psalms Speak for Us Today*. Philadelphia: The Westminster Press, 1974.

Anders-Richards, Donald. *The Drama of the Psalms*. London: Darton, Longman and Todd, 1968.

Archer, Gleason L. *A Survey of Old Testament Introduction*. Chicago: Moody Press, 1964.

Armerding, Carl. *Psalms in a Minor Key*. Chicago: Moody Press, 1973.

Armstrong, Edyth S. *Studies in the Psalms*. Chicago: Associated Authors, 1937.

Barnes, Albert. *Notes on the Old Testament: Psalms*. 3 Vols. Grand Rapids: Baker Book House, 1950.

Barnes, William Emery. *The Psalms*. Westminster Commentaries, 2 Vols. London: Methuen and Company, Ltd., 1931.

Baron, David. *Types, Psalms and Prophecies*. New York: American Board of Missions to the Jews, Inc., n.d.

Baroody, Anees T. *The Syrian Shepherd*. Chicago: Privately printed, 1916.

Barth, Christoph F. *Introduction to the Psalms*. Translated by R. A. Wilson. New York: Charles Scribner's Sons, 1966.

Barthelemy, D. and J. T. Milik. *Qumran Cave I. Discoveries in the Judaean Desert, I*. Oxford: 1955.

Baxter, J. Sidlow. *Explore the Book*. Vol. III. Grand Rapids: Zondervan Publishing House, 1960.

Binnie, William. *The Psalms: Their History, Teachings, and Use*. London: Hodder and Stoughton, 1886.

Birkeland, H. *The Evildoers in the Book of Psalms*. Oslo: J. Dybwad, 1955.

Briggs, Charles Augustus and Emilie G. Briggs. *The Book of Psalms*. Vol. I. New York: Charles Scribner's Sons, 1914.

Briscoe, Stuart. *What Works When Life Doesn't*. Wheaton: Victor Books, 1967.

Brown, Francis, S. R. Driver and Charles Briggs. *A Hebrew and English Lexicon*. Oxford: The Clarendon Press, 1952.

Bruce, F. F. *This . . . is That*. Devon: Paternoster Press, 1968.

Brumfield, J. C. *Potter and the Shepherd*. Wheaton: Van Kampen Press, n.d.

Burgh, William de. *Commentary on the Book of Psalms*. Dublin: Hodges, Smith, 1860.

Bush, G. *A Commentary on the Book of Psalms*. New York: Leavitt, Lord and Company, 1834.

Bythner, Victorinus. *The Lyre of David*. London: Whittaker and Company, 1847.

Canney, Maurice A. *Ancient Concepts of Kingship. Oriental Studies in Honour of Cursetji Pavry*. London: Oxford Press, 1953.

Cansdale, George. *All the Animals of the Bible Lands*. Grand Rapids: Zondervan Publishing House, 1970.

Clark, R. T. Rundle. *Myth and Symbol in Ancient Egypt*. London: Thames and Hudson, 1959.

Clarke, Arthur G. *Analytical Studies in the Psalms*. Kansas City, Kansas: Walterick Publishers, 1949.

Cohen, A. (ed.). *The Psalms*. London: The Soncino Press, 1968.

_____. *The Psalms: Hebrew Text and English Translation and Commentary*. London: The Soncino Press, 1968.

Dahood, Mitchell. *Psalms I (1-50). The Anchor Bible*. Garden City, New York: Doubleday and Company, Inc., 1966.

_____. *Ugaritic-Hebrew Philology*. Rome: Pontifical Biblical Institute, 1965.

Daniel, R. E. *How to Study the Psalms*. New York: Revell, 1953.

Delitzsch, Franz. *Biblical Commentary on the Psalms*. Vol. I. Grand Rapids: Wm. B. Eerdmans Publishing Company, n.d.

de Vaux, Roland. *Ancient Israel*. New York: McGraw-Hill Book Company, 1965.

DeWitt, John. *The Psalms*. New York: Anson D. F. Randolph and Company, 1891.

Dickson, David. *A Commentary on the Psalms.* London: Banner of Truth Trust, 1966.

Dyke, Henry van. *The Story of the Psalms.* New York: Charles Scribner's Sons, 1887.

Eerdmans, B. D. *Essays on Masoretic Psalms. Oudtestamentische Studien.* Leiden: E. J. Brill, 1942.

Evans, William. *The Shepherd Psalm.* Chicago: Moody Press, 1921.

Fauna and Flora of the Bible. London: United Bible Societies, 1972.

Faw, C. E. *Royal Motifs in the Hebrew Psalter.* Chicago: University of Chicago Libraries, 1939.

Forbes, John. *Studies on the Book of Psalms.* Edinburgh: T. and T. Clark. 1888.

Freed, Edwin D. *Old Testament Quotations in the Gospel of John. Supplements to Novum Testamentum XI.* Leiden: E. J. Brill, 1965.

Freehof, Solomon. *The Book of Psalms.* Union of American Hebrew Congregations, 1938.

Furneaux, W. M. *The Book of Psalms.* New York: George H. Doran Company, 1923.

Gaebelein, A. C. *The Book of Psalms.* Neptune, New Jersey: Loizeaux Brothers, 1939.

Gemser, Berend, *et al. Studies in the Psalms.* Leiden: E. J. Brill, 1963.

Gevirtz, S. *Patterns in the Early Poetry of Israel.* SAOC 32. Chicago: University of Chicago Press, 1963.

Glueck, Nelson. *Hesed in the Bible.* Edited by Elias L. Epstein. Translated by Alfred Gottschalk. New York: Ktav Publishing House, 1975.

Gordon, Cyrus H. *Ugaritic Textbook: Glossary and Indices.* Rome: Pontificium Institutum Biblicum, 1967.

Gunn, George S. *God in the Psalms*. Edinburgh: The Saint Andrews Press, 1956.

Heaton, Eric Wm. *Everyday Life in Old Testament Times*. New York: Charles Scribner's Sons, 1956.

Henderson, George. *The Pearl of Psalms*. Edinburgh: B. McCall Barbour, n.d.

Herder, J. G. *The Spirit of Hebrew Poetry*. Burlington: E. Smith, 1833.

Horn, Siegfried H. *Seventh-day Adventist Bible Dictionary*. Washington, D.C.: Review and Herald, 1960.

Hulley, L. *Studies in the Book of Psalms*. New York: Revell, 1906.

Inch, Morris A. *Psychology in the Psalms*. Waco, Texas: Word Books, 1969.

Ironside, Henry A. *Studies on Book One of the Psalms*. New York: Loizeaux Brothers, 1952.

Johnson, Aubrey R. *Psalm 23 and the Household of Faith*. Proclamation and Presence, edited by J. I. Durham and J. R. Porter. Richmond: John Knox Press, 1970.

_____. *Sacral Kingship in Ancient Israel*. Cardiff: University of Wales Press, 1967.

Keel, Othmar. *The Symbolism of the Biblical World*. New York: A Crossroad Book, The Seabury Press, 1978.

Keller, Phillip. *A Shepherd Looks at Psalm 23*. Grand Rapids: Zondervan Publishing House, 1970.

Ketcham, Robert T. *I Shall Not Want*. Chicago: Moody Press, 1953.

Kidner, Derek. *Psalms 1-72. The Tyndale Old Testament Commentaries,* edited by D. J. Wiseman. London: The Tyndale Press, 1968.

Knight, W. A. *The Song of Our Syrian Guest*. Stirling, Scotland: Stirling Tract Enterprise, n.d.

Knudtzon, J. A. *Die El-Amarna-Tafeln, I.* Aalen: Otto Zeller Verlagsbuchhandlung, 1964.

Koehler, Ludwig and Walter Baumgartner. *Lexicon in Veteris Testamenti Libros.* Leiden: E. J. Brill, 1958.

Leupold, H. C. *Exposition of the Psalms.* Minneapolis: Augsburg Publishing House, 1959.

Lewis, Clives S. *Reflections on the Psalms.* New York: Harcourt, Brace and Company, 1958.

Luckenbill, D. D. *Ancient Records of Assyria and Babylonia.* Chicago: University of Chicago Press, 1926.

Mackie, George M. *Bible Manners and Customs.* New York: Fleming H. Revell Company, n.d.

Maclaren, A. *The Psalms. The Expositor's Bible,* edited by W. Robertson Nicoll. Vol. I. New York: Funk and Wagnalls Company, 1900.

M'Clintock, John and James Strong. *Cyclopaedia of Biblical, Theological and Ecclesiastical Literature.* Vol. IX. Grand Rapids: Baker Book House, Reprinted, 1970.

McNeill, John. *The Twenty-third Psalm.* Fleming H. Revell Company, 1927.

Meek, Theophile, trans. *The Code of Hammurabi. Ancient Near Eastern Texts,* edited by James B. Pritchard. Princeton: Princeton University Press, 1955.

Meyer, F. B. *Meyer on the Psalms.* Grand Rapids: Zondervan Publishing House, n.d.

――――. *The Shepherd Psalm.* New York: H. M. Caldwell Company, n.d.

Mountford, Lydia Mary Olive. *King of the Shepherds and His Psalm.* Cincinnati: Abingdon Press, n.d.

Muilenburg, J. *The Psalms. A Form-Critical Introduction.* Philadelphia: Fortress Press, 1967.

Oesterley, W. O. E. *The Psalms.* London: S. P. C. K., 1962.

Owen, G. F. *The Shepherd Psalm of Palestine.* Grand Rapids: Wm. B. Eerdmans Publishing Company, 1958.

Perowne, J. J. Stewart. *The Book of Psalms,* Vol. I. Grand Rapids: Zondervan Publishing House, 1966.

Petersham, M. S. *The Shepherd Psalm.* New York: Macmillan, 1962.

Pettingill, W. L. *Christ in the Psalms.* Findlay, Ohio: Fundamental Truth, 1937.

Phillips. O. E. *Exploring the Messianic Psalms.* Philadelphia: Hebrew Christian Fellowship, Inc., 1967.

Plumer, William S. *Studies in the Book of Psalms.* Philadelphia: J. B. Lippincott and Company, 1866.

Prothero, R. E. *The Psalms in Human Life.* New York: E. P. Dutton, 1930.

Rappoport, A. S. *The Psalms in Life, Legend and Literature.* London: The Centenary Press, 1935.

Redding, David A. *Psalms of David.* Westwood, New Jersey: Fleming H. Revell Company, 1963.

Ringgren, Helmer. *Religions of the Ancient Near East.* Philadelphia: Westminster, 1973.

Scroggie, W. Graham. *The Psalms.* Old Tappan, New Jersey: Fleming H. Revell Company, 1965.

Shiloh, Ailon. *Peoples and Cultures of the Middle East.* New York: Random House, 1969.

Smith, J. M. Powis. *The Psalms.* Chicago: The University of Chicago Press, 1926.

Smith, R. O. *Meditations on the Psalms.* New York: William Frederich Press, 1956.

Snaith, Norman H. *Studies in the Psalter.* London: Epworth Press, 1934.

Spurgeon, Charles H. *Psalms.* Grand Rapids: Kregel Publications, 1968.

_____. *The Treasury of David.* New York: Funk and Wagnalls, 1892.

Stalker, James. *The Psalm of Psalms.* New York: Charles Scribner's Sons, 1913.

Stedman, Ray C. *Folk Psalms of Faith.* Glendale, California: Regal Books, 1973.

Stoddart, J. *The Psalms for Every Day.* Nashville: Cokesbury, 1940.

Taylor, Isaac. *The Spirit of the Hebrew Poetry.* London: Bell and Daldy, 1861.

Taylor, William R. and W. Stewart McCullough. "Psalms." *Interpreter's Bible,* edited by George A. Buttrick, Vol. IV. New York: Abingdon Press, 1955.

Thompson, J. G. S. S. "Book of Psalms." *The New Bible Dictionary,* edited by J. D. Douglas. Grand Rapids: Wm. B. Eerdmans Publishing Company, 1962.

Thomson, W. M. *The Land and the Book.* London: T. Nelson and Sons, 1903.

Weiss, C. Christian. *Insights Into Bible Times and Customs.* Lincoln, Nebraska: Back to the Bible Broadcast, 1972.

Weir, C. J. Mullo. "Letters from Tell El-Amarna." *Documents from Old Testament Times,* edited by D. Winton Thomas. New York: Harper and Row, 1961.

Wright, Fred H. *Manners and Customs of Bible Lands.* Chicago: Moody Press, 1953.

Young, E. J. *Introduction to the Old Testament.* Grand Rapids: Wm. B. Eerdmans Publishing Company, 1949.

Articles

Alden, Robert L. "Chiastic Psalms: A Study in the Mechanics of Semitic Poetry in Psalms 1-50." *Journal of the Evangelical Theological Society* 17 (1974).

Ammassari, A. "Il Salmo 23." *Bibbia e Oriente* 16 (1974).

Asensio, F. "Entre cruce de simbolos y realidades en el Salmo 23." *Biblica* 9 (1928).

Aytoun, R. A. "Psalm 23:6 and the Hound of Heaven." *Expository Times* 28 (1916-17).

Bishop, Eric F. F. "The Door of the Sheep." *Expository Times* 71 (1960).

Black, A. "The Twenty Third Psalms." *Expository Times* 10 (1899).

Blidstein, G. J. "Nature in Psalms." *Judaism* 13 (1964).

Boessneck, Joachim and Angela von den Driesch. "Preliminary Analysis of the Animal Bones from Ḥesbân." *Andrews University Seminary Studies* 16 (1978).

Braunstein, Richard. "The Green Thought." *The Expositor* 23 (1932).

Brownlee, William H. "Ezekiel's Poetic Indictment of the Shepherds." *Harvard Theological Review* 51 (1958).

Carver, D. "Nature in the Psalms." *Review and Expositor* 28 (1931).

Dahood, Mitchell. "Congruity of Metaphors." *Vetus Testamentum Supplement* 16 (1967).

Davis, John J. "Jordan's Badia Patrol: Dust and Danger." *Warsaw Times-Union.* August 5, 1976.

de Moor, J. C. "Rapi-uma-Rephaim." *Zeitschrift für die Alttestamentliche Wissenschaft* 88 (1976).

Devilliers, J. L. "The Shepherd and his flock." *The Christ of John. Neotestamentica 2.* Potchefstroom, South Africa: Pro Rege Press, 1971.

Drum, W. "Translation of Psalm 22:5." *American Ecclesiastical Review* 55 (1916).

Emden, C. S. "Psalmist's Emphasis on God's Kindness." *Church Quarterly Review,* 156 (1955).

Emerton, J. A. "Interpretation of Psalm LXXXII in John X." *Journal of Theological Studies* 11 (1960).

_____. "Melchizedek and the Gods: Fresh Evidence for the Jewish Background of John X:34-36 (cf. to Ps. LXXXII)." *Journal of Theological Studies* 17 (1966).

Fisher, Loren R. "Betrayed by Friends: an Expository Study of Psalm 22." *Interpretation* 18 (1964).

Frost, Stanley Brice. "Psalm 22: An Exposition." *Canadian Journal of Theology* 8 (1962).

Gese, Hartmut. "Psalm 22 and the New Testament." *Theology Digest* 18 (1970).

Gluck, J. J. "Nagid-Shepherd." *Vetus Testamentum* 13 (1963).

Goodman, A. E. "*hsd* and *twdh* in the Linguistic Tradition of the Psalter." *Words and Meanings, Essays Presented to D. Winton Thomas.* Edited by Peter Ackroyd and Barnabas Linaders. Cambridge: University Press, 1968.

Goodspeed, G. S. "The Twenty-Fourth Psalm." *Old and New Testament Student* 9 (1889).

Hamilton, G. F. "Psalm 23." *Expository Times* 17 (1905-06).

Hamilton, V. P. "The Shepherd Psalm: Psalm 23." *Asbury Seminarian,* 26 (1972).

Haupt, P. "The Poetic Form of Psalm 23." *American Journal of Semitic Languages and Literature* 21 (1905).

Hovey, A. "The Twenty-Second Psalm." *Biblical World* 22 (1903).

Ishida, Tomoo. "The Leaders of the Tribal League 'Israel' in the Pre-Monarchic Period." *Revue Biblique* 80 (1973).

Kelley, Sidney. "Psalm 24: A Study in Imagery." *Journal of Biblical Literature* 89 (1970).

Koehler, L. "Psalm 23." *Zeitschrift für die Alttestamentliche Wissenschaft* 68 (1956).

Lane, G. Eric. "The Good Shepherd and His Sheep." *Bible League Quarterly* 295 (1973).

Lang, M. B. "The Beatitudes in the Twenty-third Psalm." *Expository Times* 10 (1898-99).

Laurin, R. B. "The Meaning of Chesedh." *Foundations* 7 (1964).

Lawrence, Thomas G. "The Shepherd Psalm." *Sunday School Times and Gospel Herald* 72 (1974).

Martin, W. J. "Shepherd Psalm: Patterns of Freedom." *Christianity Today* 12 (1968).

Martin, W. W. "Thirty-third Psalm as an Alphabetical Psalm: A Reconstruction." *American Journal of Semitic Languages and Literature* 41 (1925).

Milne, Pamela. "Psalm 23: Echoes of the Exodus." *Sciences Religieuses* 4 (1974/75).

Morgenstern, Julian. "Psalm 23." *Journal of Biblical Literature* 65 (1946).

Owen, J. J. "The Yahweh Psalm (Psalm 23.)" *Review and Expositor* 42 (1947).

Panosian, E. M. "The Psalms: An Anatomy of All Parts of the Soul." *Biblical Viewpoint* 4 (1970).

Postgate, J. N. "Some Old Babylonian Shepherds and Their Flocks." *Journal of Semitic Studies* 20 (1975).

Power, E. "The Shepherd's Two Rods in Modern Palestine and Some Passages of the Old Testament." *Biblica* (1928).

Quasten, J. "The Parable of the Shepherd." *Catholic Biblical Quarterly* 10 (1948).

Robinson, John A. T. "The Parable of John 10:1-5." *Zeitschrift für die Neutestamentliche Wissenschaft* 46 (1955).

Schneider, Johannes. "Zur komposition von Joh. 10." *Coniectanea Neotestamentica in honorem Antoni Fridrichsen* XI (1947).

Simon, J. "The Good Shepherd Psalm." *American Ecclesiastical Review* 55 (1916).

Simpson, B. F. "An Exegesis of the Twenty-third Psalm." *Old Testament Student* 3 (1883-84).

Smith, G. A. "Psalm 23." *Expository Times* 1 (1895).

Steese, P. "Herbert and Crasaw: Two Paraphrases of the Twenty-Third Psalm." *Journal of Bible and Religion* 33 (1965).

Stuart, M. "A Word More on Psalm 22:17." *Bibliotheca Sacra* 9 (1852).

Thomas, D. W. "Salmawet in the Old Testament." *Journal of Semitic Studies* (1962).

Trudinger, Paul. "The Word on the Generation Gap. Reflections on a Gospel Metaphor." *Biblical Theology Bulletin* 5 (1975).

Vogt, Ernest. "The 'Place in Life' of Ps 23." *Biblica* 32 (1953).

Volz, P. "Psalm 23." *Neue Kirchliche Zeitschrift* 36 (1925).

von Rohr Sauer, Alfred. "Fact and Image in the Shepherd Psalm." *Concordia Theological Monthly* 42 (1971).

Walker, D. A. "Realism in Psalm 23:1-3." *Biblical World* 2 (1893).

Whiting, John D. "Among the Bethlehem Shepherds." *National Geographic Magazine* (1926).

Wier, T. H. "Psalm 23:5." *Expository Times* 27 (1915-16).

Indexes